A Quote a Day to Find Your Way

Quotes & Thoughts to Inspire You on Your Journey

Compiled and Edited by

Melissa Eshleman

Original Edition

Find Your Way Publishing, Inc.
PO BOX 667
Norway, Maine

A Quote a Day to Find Your Way:
Quotes and Thoughts to Inspire You on Your Journey

Copyright © 2013 Melissa Eshleman
Find Your Way Publishing paperback edition, 2013

Find Your Way Publishing, Inc.
PO BOX 667
Norway, ME 04268 U.S.A.
Orders at www.findyourwaypublishing.com

Find Your Way Publishing, Inc.
First Edition, 2013

ISBN-13: 978-0-9849322-2-1
ISBN-10: 0-9849322-2-4

Library of Congress Control Number: 2013934086

A quote a day to find your way: quotes and thoughts to inspire on your journey / edited and compiled by Melissa Eshleman – 1st Ed
        p   cm
Includes index
        Summary A collection of quotations
        ISBN: 978-0-9849322-2-1
        1. Quotations, English 2. Title: A quote a day to find your
        way 3.Eshleman, Melissa

Designed by Kimberly Martin at Self-pub by Jera Publishing

Printed in the United States of America.

Dedication

This book is dedicated to all who are growing, moving forward, and making positive changes in their own lives, and in the lives of others.

About this book

"I pick my favorite quotations and store them in
my mind as ready armor, offensive or defensive,
amid the struggle of this turbulent existence."

ROBERT BURNS

This book brings two powerful tools together: Quotes
and journaling. It's been proven that by writing things
down a part of your brain is triggered which increases
your potential for growth, development, and transforma-
tion. And it's been said that the power of quotes not only
motivate and inspire, but literally save lives.

Quotes have the power to create positive change. They
can change your perspective, thereby open doors that
beforehand appeared closed. Quotes are everywhere because they work. They motivate, encourage, and inspire.
Quotes help people feel better when they feel down, depressed, or defeated. Quotes can generate strong emotions, instantly transform ones mood, and remind us
that not only are we not alone, but that we are powerful warriors. That others before us have faced similar
feelings and challenges and have persevered. Quotes remind us of our strength.

People have been sharing their wisdom for centuries.
The wisdom of others can ignite your passion, uplift
your spirit, and motivate you to reach your full potential.

I wanted this book of quotes to be simple and easy to use, yet as effective as possible. For me, I have several books on my bookshelf that promote growth, but I haven't had the time to dedicate to them because there is so much text involved. This simple quote book is broken-up by day with a small space to journal thoughts and actions that the quote may have provoked. By bringing two helpful tools together; quotes and journaling, you will be creating and manifesting your own path with each new day.

One of my favorite quotes is:

"Everything you do is based on the choices you make. It's not your parents, your past relationships, your job, the economy, the weather, an argument, or your age that is to blame. You and only you are responsible for every decision and choice you make. Period."

UNKNOWN

A Quote a Day to Find Your Way: Quotes and Thoughts to Inspire You on Your Journey is a choice in the right direction. Have fun with this and remember:

"If we all did things we are capable of doing, we would literally astound ourselves."

THOMAS EDISON

A Quote a Day to Find Your Way

Quotes & Thoughts to Inspire You on Your Journey

"You must find your own way.
Unless you find it yourself,
it will not be your own way
and will take you nowhere."

SRI NISARGADATTA, SPIRITUAL TEACHER

1

"Don't find fault, find a remedy."

HENRY FORD

Thoughts/Actions:

2

"If you're struggling with someone who is a drain on your energy, permit a complaint only when it is accompanied by a sincere and realistic proposal for a fix."

THAD MCILROY

Thoughts/Actions:

3

"No matter how many mistakes you make or how slow you progress, you are still way ahead of everyone who isn't trying."

ANTHONY ROBBINS

Thoughts/Actions:

4

"It's not your job to like me–it's mine."

BYRON KATIE

Thoughts/Actions:

5

"I don't forgive people because I am weak. I forgive them because I am strong enough to know that everyone makes mistakes."

UNKNOWN

Thoughts/Actions:

6

"The more you love the least deserving on your list, the more your life will change."

MIKE DOOLEY

Thoughts/Actions:

7

"Human history is the sad result of
each one looking out for himself."

JULIO CORTAZAR

Thoughts/Actions:

8

"But life lived only for oneself does not truly
satisfy men or women. There is a hunger in
Americans today for larger purposes beyond the
self."

BETTY FRIEDAN

Thoughts/Actions:

9

"When we know deep down that we're acting with
integrity despite impulses to do otherwise, we
feel gates of higher energy and inspiration open
inside of us."

DAN MILLMAN

Thoughts/Actions:

10

"You must not lose faith in humanity. Humanity is like an ocean; if a few drops of the ocean are dirty, the ocean does not become dirty."

MOHANDAS GANDHI

Thoughts/Actions:

11

"View your life with KINDSIGHT. Stop beating yourself up about things from your past. Instead of slapping your forehead and asking, "What was I thinking," Breathe and ask yourself the kinder question, "What was I learning?"

KAREN SALMANSOHN

Thoughts/Actions:

12

"Act selfless, you will be infinite."

UNKNOWN

Thoughts/Actions:

13

"The strong man is the man who can stand
up for his rights and not hit back."

MARTIN LUTHER KING, JR.

Thoughts/Actions:

14

"I have discovered that life doesn't actually knock
you down. It does, however, provide you with
many opportunities to evaluate your standing in
life: what you stand on, what you stand for, how
you stand within yourself and for yourself."

IYANLA VANZANT

Thoughts/Actions:

15

"The past is behind, learn from it.
The future is ahead, prepare for it.
The present is here, live it."

THOMAS S. MONSON

Thoughts/Actions:

16

"There are two primary choices in life: to accept conditions as they exist, or accept the responsibility for changing them."

DENIS WAITLEY

Thoughts/Actions:

17

"Yesterday is gone. Tomorrow has not yet come. We have only today. Let us begin."

MOTHER TERESA

Thoughts/Actions:

18

"The mind, once expanded to the dimensions of larger ideas, never returns to its original size."

OLIVER WENDELL HOLMES

Thoughts/Actions:

19

"I have decided to be happy, because
it's good for my health."

VOLTAIRE

Thoughts/Actions:

20

"Plenty of people miss their share of happiness.
Not because they never found it–but because they
didn't stop to enjoy it."

WILLIAM FEATHER

Don't miss your share of happiness!
Stop and enjoy THIS moment!

Thoughts/Actions:

21

"Don't mistake movement for achievement. It's
easy to get faked out by being busy. The question
is: Busy doing what?"

JIM ROHN

Thoughts/Actions:

22

This little light of mine,
I'm going to let it shine.

Let YOUR light shine!

Thoughts/Actions:

23

"Let the simple things of life warm your soul."
CATHY GIBSONSMITH

Are you letting the simple things warm your soul today? What are some of the simple things you are appreciating today?

Thoughts/Actions:

24

"Dreams are illustrations... from the book your soul is writing about you."
MARSHA NORMAN

Therefore dream BIG!

Thoughts/Actions:

25

"A good laugh overcomes more
difficulties and dissipates more dark
clouds than any other one thing."

LAURA INGALLS WILDER

Thoughts/Actions:

26

"If you want to be happy, be."

LEO TOLSTOY

Thoughts/Actions:

27

"It is always safe to assume, not that the old way
is wrong, but that there may be a better way."

HENRY F. HARROWER

Thoughts/Actions:

28

"If you really want to do
something, you'll find a way.
If you don't, you'll find an excuse."

JIM ROHN

Thoughts/Actions:

29

"Every day you have the choice of
either being a Worrier or a Warrior."

VICKI GOETZ

Thoughts/Actions:

30

"No matter how long we have traveled on the
wrong road, we can always turn around."

POSITIVELY POSITIVE

Thoughts/Actions:

31

"Never regret. If it's good, it's wonderful.
If it's bad, it's experience."

VICTORIA HOLT

Thoughts/Actions:

32

"Finish each day and be done with it. You
have done what you could; some blunders and
absurdities have crept in; forget them as soon
as you can. Tomorrow is a new day; you shall
begin it serenely and with too high a spirit to be
encumbered with your old nonsense."

RALPH WALDO EMERSON

Thoughts/Actions:

33

"Sooner or later we must realize there is no
station, no one place to arrive at, once and for
all. The true joy of life is the trip."

ROBERT J. HASTINGS

Thoughts/Actions:

34

#12 of the book "Guaranteed Success for Grade School; 50 Easy Things You Can Do Today" is: Good sportsmanship ~ Here's to playing fair and respecting others. May children & adults take pride in their accomplishments and in improving their skills, and see themselves as winners, no matter what the "scoreboard" says!

Thoughts/Actions:

35

"Now, this is the key to your Deliberate Creating: See yourself as this magnet, attracting unto you the way you feel at any point in time. When you feel clear and in control, you will attract circumstances of clarity. When you feel happy, you will attract circumstances of happiness. When you feel healthy, you will attract circumstances of health. When you feel prosperous, you will attract circumstances of prosperity. When you feel loved, you will attract circumstances of love. Literally, the way you feel is your point of attraction."

ABRAHAM HICKS

Thoughts/Actions:

36.

Five Simple Rules For Happiness:

1. Free your heart from hatred
2. Free your mind from worries
3. Live simply
4. Give more
5. Expect Less

Thoughts/Actions:

37.

"Everyone smiles in the same language."

GEORGE CARLIN

Thoughts/Actions:

38

"Nothing can bring you peace but
yourself. Nothing can bring you peace
but the triumph of principles."

RALPH WALDO EMERSON

Here's to a peaceful day!

Thoughts/Actions:

39

The Ego (False Self)	Vs.	The Soul (Real Self)
Me		We
Separation		Unity
Blame		Understanding
Hostility		Friendliness
Resentment		Forgiveness
Pride		Love
Complain		Gratefulness
Jealousy		Co-Happiness
Anger		Happiness
Power		Humble
Materialism		Spiritualism
Madness		Wisdom
War		Peace
Coldness		Sympathy
Past/Future Oriented		Now Oriented
Intolerance		Tolerance
Self-importance		We-Importance
Self-Denial		Self-Acceptance
Drama		Simplicity
Doing		Being

The secret to finding your
way... so simple really.

Thoughts/Actions:

14

40

"Today is a new day! You can start fresh wipe the slate clean and begin again. Today you can embrace kindness, practice compassion, stand up for justice, talk to strangers, ask for help, offer Hope and listen with your whole heart. Work for the common good. Love well. You can be the change you wish to see in the world."

AUTHOR UNKNOWN

Thoughts/Actions:

41

"True wealth is a byproduct of living a principled life."

GARRETT GUNDERSON

Thoughts/Actions:

42

Take responsibility. "Never ruin an apology with an excuse."

KIMBERLY JOHNSON

Thoughts/Actions:

43

"Maturity begins when we're content to feel we're right about something, without feeling the necessity to prove someone else is wrong."

SYDNEY J. HARRIS

Thoughts/Actions:

44

A Cherokee Legend

An old Cherokee is teaching his grandson about life. "A fight is going on inside me," he said to the boy.

"It is a terrible fight and it is between two wolves. One is evil–he is anger, envy, sorrow, regret, greed, arrogance, self-pity, guilt, resentment, inferiority, lies, false pride, superiority, and ego." He continued, "The other is good–he is joy, peace, love, hope, serenity, humility, kindness, benevolence, empathy, generosity, truth, compassion, and faith. The same fight is going on inside you–and inside every other person, too."

The grandson thought about it for a minute and then asked his grandfather, "Which wolf will win?"

The old Cherokee simply replied, "The one you feed."

Thoughts/Actions:

45

"Each morning we are born again. What
we do today is what matters most."

BUDDHA

Thoughts/Actions:

46

"Worry less, smile more, accept criticism, take
responsibility, listen & love, don't hate, embrace
change, and feel good anyway."

UNKNOWN

Thoughts/Actions:

47

"You decide every moment of every day who you
are and what you believe in. You get a second
chance, every second."

UNKNOWN

Thoughts/Actions:

48

Let go
Surrender
Taste Freedom

"The thing is, we have to let go of all blame, all attacking, all judging, to free our inner selves to attract what we say we want. Until we do, we are hamsters in a cage chasing our own tails and wondering why we aren't getting the results we seek."

DR. JOE VITALE

Take a moment to let go of all blame, all attacking, all judging... then another... then another... and repeat. Free yourself, love one another, & watch miracles happen!

Thoughts/Actions:

49

"The man is the richest whose pleasures are the cheapest."

HENRY DAVID THOREAU

Thoughts/Actions:

50

"The lens that you wear to interpret your situation, with either move you towards the truth of your soul, or the lies of your ego."

AUTHOR UNKNOWN

Thoughts/Actions:

51

"Creativity is allowing yourself to make mistakes. Art is knowing which ones to keep."

SCOTT ADAMS

Mistakes can be easily made. Trial & error. When you make mistakes, learn from them but don't keep them.

Thoughts/Actions:

52

"Enjoy simple pleasures. Truly, the best pleasures in life are free."

Author Unknown

WHAT ARE YOUR SIMPLE PLEASURES?

Thoughts/Actions:

53

A good list to live by
and remember:

The most destructive habit...

Worry

The greatest joy...

Giving

The greatest loss...

Self-respect

The most satisfying work...

Helping Others

The ugliest personality trait...

Selfishness

The most endangered species...

Dedicated leaders

Our greatest natural resource...

Our youth

The greatest "shot in the arm"...

Encouragement

The greatest problem to overcome...

Fear

The most effective sleeping pill...

Peace of mind

The most crippling failure disease...

Excuses

The most powerful force in life...

Love

The most dangerous outcast...

A gossip

The world's most incredible computer…

The brain

The worst thing to be without…

Hope

The deadliest weapon…

The tongue

The two most power-filled words…

"I can"

The greatest asset…

Faith

The most worthless emotion…

Self-pity

The most beautiful attire…

A Smile

The most prized possession…

Integrity

The most contagious spirit…

Enthusiasm

The most powerful channel of communication . . .

Prayer

Thoughts/Actions:

54

"Tempests exist only to test your foundation."
AUTHOR UNKNOWN

How strong is your foundation? If it's weak, that's
an indicator that it just needs attention and

maybe a little patch work. If it's broken, it needs rebuilding. Here's to finding our way to integrity, strength, love, and strong foundations!

"Because if you have a strong foundation, then you can build or rebuild anything on it. But if you've got a weak foundation you can't build anything."

JACK SCALIA

Thoughts/Actions:

55

"Don't quit! Do it! Every difficulty is an opportunity in disguise."

AUTHOR UNKNOWN

Thoughts/Actions:

56

"Every day is a new beginning. All of life provides opportunities for new beginnings. Whatever has gone wrong, or right, in your life, you can begin again."

UNKNOWN

Every day is a new day! Each day we can start again moving towards what matters most. Appreciate that while appreciating yourself and have a wonderful day!

Thoughts/Actions:

57

"Plant seeds of happiness, hope, success, and love; it will all come back to you in abundance. This is the law of nature."

STEVE MARABOLI

Thoughts/Actions:

58

"Treat everyone with politeness, even those who are rude to you–not because they are nice, but because you are."

AUTHOR UNKNOWN

Thoughts/Actions:

59

"Smiling's my favorite!"

BUDDY THE ELF

Did you know that even when you fake a smile you feel better? It's true because smiling releases endorphins! So smile at everyone & everything and start feeling great today!

Thoughts/Actions:

60

"The person who says it cannot be done should not interrupt the person doing it."

CHINESE PROVERB

Thoughts/Actions:

61

"For any of us...to find the universal elements enough... to find the air and the water exhilarating...to be refreshed by a morning walk...or an evening saunter ... to be thrilled by the stars at night....to be elated over a wildflower in spring...these are some of the rewards of listening to our own hearts...of reconnecting with the simple joys...that are always available in the days that make up our lifetimes..."

JOHN BURROUGHS

Thoughts/Actions:

62

"The ultimate measure of a man is not where he stands in moments of comfort and convenience, but where he stands at times of challenge and controversy."

MARTIN LUTHER KING JR.

Thoughts/Actions:

63

"When looking for the path to peace, one comes to realize–Peace IS the path."

UNKNOWN

Have a peaceful day!

Thoughts/Actions:

64

"In life, it's not where you go—
It's who you travel with."

UNKNOWN

Thoughts/Actions:

65

"When nothing goes right.... Go left."

AUTHOR UNKNOWN

Thoughts/Actions:

66

"The minute you expose darkness to the light, the light begins to defeat it. The darkness then loses its power over you."

JOYCE MEYER

Thoughts/Actions:

67

"We do not want to gain at someone else's loss; we want to gain while helping the other person to also gain."

JOSE SILVA

Thoughts/Actions:

68

"Effort is only effort when it begins to hurt."

JOSE ORTEGA Y GASSET

Thoughts/Actions:

69

"Every man is guilty of all the good he did not do."

VOLTAIRE

Thoughts/Actions:

70

"When a person can find the gift within the trial, then the trial will have served its purpose. It's when we flounder through the same type of trial over and over and never learn anything, never find the gift, that we keep going through the same, seemingly fruitless struggles."

ANITA STANSFIELD

Thoughts/Actions:

71

"Learn to get in touch with the silence within yourself, and know that everything in life has purpose. There are no mistakes, no coincidences, all events are blessings given to us to learn from."

ELISABETH KUBLER-ROSS

Thoughts/Actions:

72

The difference between a helping hand and
an outstretched palm is a twist of the wrist.

LAURENCE LEAMER, KING OF THE NIGHT

Thoughts/Actions:

73

"Life is a sum of all your choices."

ALBERT CAMUS

"Everything you do is based on the choices
you make. It's not your parents, your past
relationships, your job, the economy, the weather,
an argument, or your age that is to blame. You
and only you are responsible for every decision
and choice you make, period."

UNKNOWN

Point the finger of responsibility back to yourself,
and away from others when you are discussing
the consequences of your actions, and you will
free yourself to move forward in a positive
direction. Here's to taking responsibility for all
of our choices, learning from them, and moving
forward toward our dreams.

Thoughts/Actions:

74

"Some quit due to slow progress. Never grasping the fact that slow progress....IS progress."

UNKNOWN

Thoughts/Actions:

75

"As your faith is strengthened you will find that there is no longer the need to have a sense of control, that things will flow as they will, and that you will flow with them, to your great delight and benefit."

EMMANUEL TENEY

Thoughts/Actions:

76

"Turn your face to the sun and the shadows fall behind you."

MAORI PROVERB

Thoughts/Actions:

77

"Being happy isn't about WHAT you have.
It's about the THOUGHTS you have."

NOTSALMON.COM

You get to choose. Choose your
thoughts today and be happy! :)

Thoughts/Actions:

78

"If you are trapped between your feelings and
what other people think is right, always go for
whatever makes you happy. Unless, you want
everybody to be happy except you".

UNKNOWN

Thoughts/Actions:

79

"There is only one happiness in
this life, to love and be loved."

GEORGE SAND

Thoughts/Actions:

80

"The flower of consciousness needs
the mud out of which it grows."
ECKART TOLLE

Remember you need the mud in order to grow. "Mud" is useful and needed. When you're feeling down or confused, don't get stuck in the "mud"; feel it, learn from it, and then move through it. Be aware that "mud" is a tool to help you appreciate and expand. ♥

Mondays are an example of this. The muddiness of Mondays is what helps you appreciate the freeing awesomeness of Fridays. Without Monday, you wouldn't appreciate Friday nearly as much. :)

Thoughts/Actions:

81

"For myself I am an optimist — it does not
seem to be much use being anything else."
WINSTON CHURCHILL

Thoughts/Actions:

82

"What a liberation to realize that the "voice in my head" is not who I am. Who am I then? The one who sees that."

ECKHART TOLLE

How do you silence the ego? By recognizing and trusting the simplicity of it. And by making it fun. Quieting the mind can be simple if you believe it to be so. When you find yourself thinking, worrying or judging; decide that you don't have to think those thoughts right now. Replace those thoughts with something that represents calm for you. A candle flame, a cloud, a sunset, it can even be a word like "love" or "peace"; whatever works for you. Always go back to that image or word. Before you know it, you will be a master at quieting your mind and the all-knowing wisdom that is within you, and always has been, will emerge and give you all the answers you're looking for. You will never have to look outside yourself for answers or validation because everything you need to know is within. Stop thinking, stop judging, and stop worrying; quiet the mind, meditate, be still, be in the present, and allow your knowingness to come into full fruition. And have fun with it. Your inner self wants you to. :)

Thoughts/Actions:

83

"The trick is to enjoy life. Don't wish away your days, waiting for better ones ahead. The grand and the simple. They are equally wonderful."

MARJORIE PAY HINCKLEY

Thoughts/Actions:

84

I am strong because I am weak.
I am beautiful because I know my flaws.
I am a lover because I am a fighter.
I am fearless because I have been afraid.
I am wise because I have been foolish.
And I can laugh because I've known sadness.

UNKNOWN

Thoughts/Actions:

85

"To argue with a person who has renounced the use of reason is like administering medicine to the dead."

THOMAS PAINE

There's no use. Never waste your
precious time or energy arguing.

Thoughts/Actions:

86

"If we all do one random act of
kindness daily, we just might set the
world in the right direction."

MARTIN KORNFELD

Do you do random acts of kindness each day?

Thoughts/Actions:

87

"The whole Zen attitude is to bring to your notice
the fact that there is no effort to be made. The
Zen attitude is that of effortlessness."

OSHO

Thoughts/Actions:

88

"If you can find a path with no obstacles,
it probably doesn't lead anywhere."

FRANK A. CLARK

Obstacles can lead to growth & appreciation.

Thoughts/Actions:

89

"Day by day, step by step, I become a little more
unbroken. And though sometimes I fall...I'm
forever falling forward."

EDDE JAE

Thoughts/Actions:

90

"I'm letting go of negative feelings, memories,
thoughts and people in my life. I have no room
for them. And will only think positive, happy
thoughts from now on."

AUTHOR UNKNOWN

You're the only one who can do this.
You're in control. And you've got this!

Thoughts/Actions:

91

Simplicity: "Don't make the
process harder than it is."
JACK WELCH

"Life is Simple—Eat – Sleep–Love"
UNKNOWN

It doesn't have to be difficult. Life is simple. Eat,
Sleep, Love. Most of us have the first two figured
out, but let's not forget, all three come naturally.
Can you do it? Can you extend love to every person
on the planet? Including yourself of course. Love is
what we were born with. We were born as loving,
nonjudgmental beings. Let's unlearn some of the
programs we've been taught. Life is simple. Eat,
Sleep, Love.

Thoughts/Actions:

92

"Choose being kind over being right,
and you'll be right every time."
RICHARD CARLSON

Thoughts/Actions:

93

"What you allow is what will continue."

UNKNOWN

Thoughts/Actions:

94

"Inner peace can be reached only when we practice forgiveness. Forgiveness is letting go of the past, and is therefore the means for correcting our misperceptions. "

GERALD JAMPOLSKY

Inner peace is the goal. Forgiveness. Letting go of the past. What we think isn't always so, therefore, becoming aware and/or correcting our misperceptions is the door to peace, and ultimately love. And forgive yourself, for these misperceptions are just what they are misperceptions, and they are not real. Here's to peace.

Thoughts/Actions:

95

"Look at everything as though you were seeing it either for the first or last time. Then your time on earth will be filled with glory."

BETTY SMITH

Try to do this for one hour, then
one day, then two, etc.

Thoughts/Actions:

96

"Help others achieve their dreams and you will achieve yours."–Les Brown

Thoughts/Actions:

97

"Darkness cannot drive out darkness: only light can do that. Hate cannot drive out hate: only love can do that."

MARTIN LUTHER KING JR.

Thoughts/Actions:

98

"When the power of love overcomes the love of power, the world will know peace."

JIMI HENDRIX

Thoughts/Actions:

99

"I cried because I had no shoes. Then I met a man who had no feet. Life is full of blessings. Sometimes we're just blind to see them."

WALLY LAMB

Thoughts/Actions:

100

"One of the most tragic things I know about human nature is that all of us tend to put off living. We are all dreaming of some magical rose garden over the horizon–instead of enjoying the roses that are blooming outside our windows today."

DALE CARNEGIE

Thoughts/Actions:

101

"Wake up every morning with the thought that something wonderful is about to happen."

UNKNOWN

Thoughts/Actions:

102

"You will only begin to heal when you let go of past hurts, forgive those who have wronged you and learn to forgive yourself for your mistakes."

UNKNOWN

Thoughts/Actions:

103

"Our prime purpose in this life is to help others. And if you can't help them, at least don't hurt them."

DALAI LAMA

Thoughts/Actions:

104

"The bad news is time flies. The
good news is you're the pilot."

MICHAEL ALTHSULER

Thoughts/Actions:

105

Five Rules to Live a Happier Life

RUBYANNE

1. Love Yourself
2. Do Good
3. Always Forgive
4. Harm No One
5. Be Positive

Thoughts/Actions:

106

Be Good to You

Be Yourself... truthfully.
Accept Yourself... gratefully.
Value Yourself... completely.
Treat Yourself... generously.
Balance Yourself... harmoniously.
Bless Yourself... abundantly.

Trust Yourself... confidently.
Love Yourself... wholeheartedly.
Empower Yourself... prayerfully.
Give Yourself... enthusiastically.
Express Yourself... radiantly.
Honor Yourself... purposefully.

AUTHOR UNKNOWN

Thoughts/Actions:

107

"A good laugh and a long sleep are
the two best cures for anything."

IRISH PROVERB

Here's to more laugh & play, rest & relaxation...

Thoughts/Actions:

108

"Don't let negative and toxic people rent space
in your head. Raise the rent and kick them out!"

ROBERT TEW

"All negativity is an illusion created by the
limited mind to protect and defend itself."

AMBIKA WAUTERS

When faced with negativity, choose to let it pass
quickly and focus on the positive. Negativity is

costly in so many ways. The effects of positive thinking are beneficial in all areas of your life and will create miracles.

Thoughts/Actions:

109

"Three things in human life are important: the first is to be kind; the second is to be kind; and the third is to be kind."

HENRY JAMES

Thoughts/Actions:

110

"Laughter and tears are both responses to frustration and exhaustion . . . I myself prefer to laugh, since there is less cleaning up to do afterward."

KURT VONNEGUT, JR.

Thoughts/Actions:

111

"At any given moment you have the power to say: "This is NOT how the story is going to end."

AUTHOR UNKNOWN

Thoughts/Actions:

112

Jacob was a cheater, Peter had a temper, David had an affair, Noah got drunk, Jonah ran from God, Paul was a murderer, Gideon was insecure, Miriam was a gossiper, Martha was a worrier, Thomas was a doubter, Sara was impatient, Elijah was moody, Moses stuttered, Zaccheus was short, Abraham was old, and Lazarus was dead. Now, what's YOUR excuse? God doesn't call the qualified, He qualifies the called.

Thoughts/Actions:

113

May you always be blessed with walls for the wind. A roof for the rain. A warm cup of tea by the fire. Laughter to cheer you. Those you love near you. And all that your heart might desire."

IRISH BLESSING

Thoughts/Actions:

114

"If "Plan A" didn't work, the alphabet
has 25 more letters! Stay cool."

UNKNOWN

Thoughts/Actions:

115

Gandhi's Top 10 Fundamentals
for changing the World

Change yourself
You are in control
Forgive and let go
Without action you aren't going anywhere
Take care of this moment
EVERYONE IS HUMAN
Persist
See the good in people and help them
Be congruent, be AUTHENTIC,
be your TRUE SELF
Continue to grow and evolve

Thoughts/Actions:

116

"Go for long walks, indulge in hot baths, question
your assumptions, be kind to yourself, live for
the moment, loosen up, scream, curse the world,
count your blessings, just let go, just be."

CAROL SHIELDS

"Taking time to do nothing often brings
everything into perspective."

DOE ZANTAMATA

How often do you take time to do nothing?

117

Say this every morning upon waking up:

"Today, something wonderful will happen."

Stop thinking about what could go wrong, and start thinking about what could go right!

Thoughts/Actions:

118

"Respect your efforts, respect yourself. Self-respect leads to self-discipline. When you have both firmly under your belt, that's real power."

CLINT EASTWOOD

"It is the highest form of self-respect to admit our errors and mistakes and make amends for them. To make a mistake is only an error in judgment, but to adhere to it when it is discovered shows infirmity of character."

DALE E. TURNER

Thoughts/Actions:

119

Kindness Pass it on!

Give someone a flower. Eat lunch with someone new. Listen with your heart. Visit a sick friend. Clean a neighbor's sidewalk. Offer someone a hug. Give an unexpected gift. Make a new friend. Pick up litter along the road or in the park. Say, " Hello." Call someone who is lonely. Open a door. Cheer up a friend. Buy someone's meal. Thank a teacher. Give blood. Do one act of kindness every day. Leave a 'thank you' note. Offer your seat to someone. Tip generously. Be tolerant of others. Let another person go first. Bake cookies for emergency workers. Tutor a student. Give someone a compliment. Read to a child. Lend a helping hand. Celebrate the day. Respect others. Encourage a child. Forgive mistakes. Drive courteously. Share a smile. . .

UNKNOWN

Thoughts/Actions:

120

"If you can drive yourself crazy, you can drive yourself happy!"

UNKNOWN

Be deliberate. Take the wheel! Make the choice to start driving in the direction that benefits YOU!

121

"Trust yourself. You know more
than you think you do."

BENJAMIN SPOCK

Thoughts/Actions:

122

You have a glass. It's half full of water, and half
full of air. So technically, the glass is always full.

"A pessimist is one who makes difficulties
of opportunities. An optimist makes
opportunities of difficulties."

AUTHOR UNKNOWN

"Optimism refuses to believe that
the road ends without options."

ROBERT SCHULLER

"Optimism. It's not just a mindset, it is behavior."

LARRY ELDER

Thoughts/Actions:

123

You were created limitless. There is
nothing you cannot achieve. Nothing.

UNKNOWN

Thoughts/Actions:

124

"First they ignore you, then they laugh at
you, then they fight you, then you win."

MAHATMA GANDHI

Thoughts/Actions:

125

"We either make ourselves miserable,
or we make ourselves strong. The
amount of work is the same."

CARLOS CASTENEDA

Thoughts/Actions:

126

Everyone takes a shower to get rid of the dirt on their physical bodies. So, doesn't it only make sense to clean your mind from all of the negative garbage from the outside world.

JOHN DI LEMME

Thoughts/Actions:

127

"Be assured that the cup adds nothing to the essence of the coffee inside."

UNKNOWN

While enjoying your coffee this morning, remember it's not the cup..... it's what's inside.

Thoughts/Actions:

128

"Once you replace negative thoughts with positive ones, you'll start having positive results."

WILLIE NELSON

Thoughts/Actions:

129

"If we believe that tomorrow will be
better, we can bear a hardship today."

THICH NHAT HANH

"Sometimes you just need to give in to the
yuckiness of the day, throw your psychic hands
up in the air and trust that tomorrow will be an
improvement."

AMY SHEARN

The other day I was having a very blah kind of
day. I felt depressed and on the verge of tears, and
I really didn't have a good explanation for it. No
amount of positive quotes, or funny images could
snap me out of it, and only seemed to irritate me
more. And I realized it was okay. When did it
stop being okay to feel blah? I know it's not the
best feeling, but there has to be balance. Yin and
Yang. Everything has an opposite. Light/Dark.
Up/Down. Happy/Sad. One cannot exist without
the other. I think it's important to trust that "this
too shall pass", because it does. And to appreciate
all of it.

Thoughts/Actions:

130

"Don't wait for people to be
kind. Show them how."

UNKNOWN

"Be kind to unkind people –
they need it the most."

ASHLEIGH BRILLIANT

Thoughts/Actions:

131

"Throughout life: I've loved, I've lied, I've hurt,
I've lost, I've missed, I've trusted, I've made
mistakes. But most of all, I've learned."

UNKNOWN

Thoughts/Actions:

132

"Learning is like rowing upstream:
not to advance is to drop back."

CHINESE PROVERB

Thoughts/Actions:

133

"Never look down on anybody
unless you're helping him up."

JESSE JACKSON

Thoughts/Actions:

134

"You will meet two kinds of people in your life:
Ones who build you up and ones who tear you
down. But in the end you will thank them both."

UNKNOWN

Thoughts/Actions:

135

"Comparison is the thief of joy."

THEODORE ROOSEVELT

Thoughts/Actions:

136

"In life we do things. Some we wish we had never done. Some we wish we could replay a million times in our heads. But they all make us who we are. And in the end they shape every detail about us. If we were to reverse any of them we wouldn't be the person we are. So just live. Make mistakes. Have wonderful memories. But never ever second guess who you are. Where you have been and most importantly where it is you're going."

UNKNOWN

Just live, appreciating who you have become, and trust that you will continue to grow and evolve in the process. Live, Learn, & Love–It's that simple!

Thoughts/Actions:

137

"Live out of your imagination, not your history."

STEPHEN COVEY

"Find that magical place in your world…. and live there."

LAURA LOUKAIDES

Thoughts/Actions:

138

"Growing old is inevitable,
growing up is optional."

UNKNOWN

"Children don't worry about the past; they don't worry about the future; they simply enjoy the each and every moment of the present. Enjoy your life like a child and relish this gift."

AUTHOR UNKNOWN

Watch elementary school children coming out of school at the end of the day. The kindergarteners, first, and second graders are laughing, skipping, jumping, and smiling. The fourth, fifth, and sixth graders….. not so much. It's an interesting observation. Remind yourself to just be happy and enjoy life as young children do.

Thoughts/Actions:

139

"Don't believe everything you think."

UNKNOWN

Feel your personal power. It can be hard at times to focus on your desires and uniqueness in times of sameness. It's easy to stand with the crowd, but it takes courage and strength to stand alone. You cannot stand with those who want to define "right" and "wrong" or "good" and "bad" and expand. Most of what we believe, we've been taught and is based on OTHER people's past beliefs. Challenge your beliefs. Don't believe everything you think and assume. It's all perception and it's an illusion. Stop thinking and just be.

Thoughts/Actions:

140

"The whole problem with the world is that fools and fanatics are always so certain of themselves, but wiser people so full of doubts."

BERTRAND RUSSELL

Thoughts/Actions:

141

Top 10 Tips To Be Happy

1. Let go, forget the burdens of the past. The past cannot be changed so use it to make the future yours.

2. Be whoever you want to be. Don't live your life how other people want you to.

3. Think positively. No matter how bad a situation, something good will come from it.

4. Remember that everything happens for a reason. When the reason reveals itself, it will blow you away.

5. Change. Learn and grow as a person, become the best person you can and want to be.

6. Look after the pennies and the pounds will look after themselves. Care for the small things and the big things will happen as a result.

7. Built relationship. Form friendships, see the good in people, share your life with them and tell them all of your secrets.

8. Live your life with purpose. Set out to achieve something and do it. The feeling of accomplishment is empowering.

9. Take responsibility. Don't blame your mistakes on others; don't blame others when things don't go to plan. Accept that it happened.

10. Smile. A lot. Smiling releases endorphins that make you feel better instantly, you'll feel happier.

HAPPINESS SPREADS, SMILE. :)

UNKNOWN

Thoughts/Actions:

142

"Your journey has molded you for your greater good, and it was exactly what it needed to be. Don't think you've lost time. There is no short-cutting to life. It took each and every situation you have encountered to bring you to the now. And now is right on time."

ASHA TYSON

You haven't lived anyone else's life but your own. Don't allow yourself to judge others for what you believe to be weaknesses or strengths because you have no idea where those attributes came from in the first place. If you were to live someone else's life 24/7 from day one, you would make the same exact choices that they have made and vice versa. You would do and say the same things they have done and said. Isn't this somewhat freeing? Just sit back, relax, and trust that all souls are growing and learning at their own pace and according to plan.

Thoughts/Actions:

143

"The only way to succeed is to NOT worry about what anyone else is doing."

UNKNOWN

Thoughts/Actions:

144

"The first to apologize is the bravest.
The first to forgive is the strongest.
The first to forget is the happiest."

UNKNOWN

Thoughts/Actions:

145

"Don't try to understand everything.
Because sometimes it's not meant to be
understood, but to be accepted."

UNKNOWN

Everyone is on their own journey and you will
never understand why they do what they do, or
believe what they believe because their journey is
not yours. Grow yourself. Don't allow yourself to
be judgmental just because you don't understand,
and accept that you never will. You can't. It's not
your journey.

Thoughts/Actions:

146

Laughter, the cheapest medicine

"A merry heart doeth good like a medicine:
but a broken spirit drieth the bones."

PROVERBS 17:22 KING JAMES VERSION

Thoughts/Actions:

147

"Finish each day and be done with it. You
have done what you could. Some blunders and
absurdities no doubt crept in; forget them as
soon as you can. Tomorrow is a new day; begin it
well and serenely and with too high a spirit to be
encumbered with your old nonsense."

RALPH WALDO EMERSON

Thoughts/Actions:

148

"Be nice to yourself. It's hard to be happy
when someone's mean to you all the time."

UNKNOWN

"Be the person your dog thinks you are."
UNKNOWN

"Next time you think of beautiful things,
don't forget to count yourself in."
UNKNOWN

Thoughts/Actions:

149

"You can't help someone uphill without
getting closer to the top yourself."
CHINESE PROVERB

Thoughts/Actions:

150

"Only love stops hate. Change our
world, love your enemies."
UNKNOWN

You can do it! Really, you can!

Thoughts/Actions:

151

"We're so busy watching out for what's
just ahead of us that we don't take
time to enjoy where we are."

CALVIN & HOBBES

"One day at a time- this is enough. Do not look
back and grieve over the past, for it is gone; and
do not be troubled about the future, for it has
not yet come. Live in the present, and make it
so beautiful that it will be worth remembering."

IDA SCOTT TAYLOR

Thoughts/Actions:

152

"Every second is a chance to
turn your life around."

UNKNOWN

Thoughts/Actions:

153

"When writing the story of your life,
don't let anyone else hold the pen."

UNKNOWN

Thoughts/Actions:

154

"I have forgiven everyone. I forgive myself. I do not harbor any resentment, contempt against anyone in my heart. I am free."

UNKNOWN

Thoughts/Actions:

155

"Leave the past in the past."

UNKNOWN

"When the past calls, let it go to voicemail. It has nothing new to say."

UNKNOWN

Today is a NEW day! Make it great!

Thoughts/Actions:

156

"The grass is greener where you water it."

UNKNOWN

What areas in your life are you watering? You have a choice. Don't allow yourself to get distracted. Be deliberate and be sure to "water" the areas of your life that are most important to YOU!

157

"Life appears to me too short to be spent in nursing animosity, or registering wrongs."

UNKNOWN

There is no us versus them. You cannot solve problems by fighting against anyone or anything. Avoid judging others as being wrong. We are all connected. When you hurt someone else or hold grudges, you are hurting yourself. It's out of the question because we are violating ourselves. So, forgive others. Rather than looking for faults in others, look for the good in them. Be kind and compassionate.

AMIT GOSWAMI

Thoughts/Actions:

158

Listen to the voice that speaks inside.

"There Is A Voice Inside Of You
That Whispers All Day Long,
"I Feel That This Is Right For Me,
I Know That This Is Wrong."
No Teacher, Preacher, Parent, Friend

Or Wise Man Can Decide
What's Right For You- Just Listen To
The Voice That Speaks Inside."

SHEL SILVERSTEIN

No teacher, preacher, parent, friend or wise man
can decide what's right for you..... just listen

Thoughts/Actions:

159

"If you want to be sad, no one in the world can
make you happy. But if you make up your mind to
be happy, no one and nothing on earth can take
that happiness from you."

P. YOGANANDA

Recognize how you are choosing to feel.
Make up your mind to be happy!

Thoughts/Actions:

160

"If you light a lamp for someone else,
it will also brighten your path."

BUDDHA

Thoughts/Actions:

161

Inside your comfort zone lies:
90% of the population
Mediocre Life
Just Survival
Fear
Tiredness
Depression
Settling
Average
What if I can't

Outside your comfort zone lies:
Fearless
Excitement
Success
Financial Freedom
Wealth
Dream
Belief
Confidence
Passion
What if I CAN

Fulfillment
The Sky is the Limit!

Try to step out of your comfort zone once in a while and amazing things will happen. You will find your way to YOU!

Thoughts/Actions:

162

"We are the result of 4 billion years
of evolution. Time to act like it."

UNKNOWN

We are the result of 4 billion years of evolutionary
success. Let's act like it! Let's love and respect
this planet we live on. Let's love one another
regardless of our warped judgments. Let's free
ourselves from the limiting "beliefs" that we've
most likely learned from others. With practice
and awareness this becomes easy. Anytime you
find yourself judging yourself or someone or
something, replace the thought with compassion,
love, and acceptance. Simple.

Thoughts/Actions:

163

"Advice is what we ask for when we already
know the answer but wish we didn't."

ERICA JONG

Quiet yourself for five seconds & listen,
because you already know the answer.

Thoughts/Actions:

164

"When I was five years old, my mother always told me that happiness was the key to life. When I went to school, they asked me what I wanted to be when I grew up. I wrote down 'happy'. They told me I didn't understand the assignment, and I told them they didn't understand life."

JOHN LENNON

"There is no key to happiness.
The door is always open."

MOTHER TERESA

"Success is not the key to happiness.
Happiness is the key to success."

ALBERT SCHWEITZER

Thoughts/Actions:

165

"Life is short, so don't hold back. Forgive like you have amnesia, believe like a kid, love like crazy, and be yourself."

UNKNOWN

Thoughts/Actions:

166

"It doesn't matter if the glass is half empty or half full. Be thankful that you have a glass and grateful that there's something in it."

UNKNOWN

"What if today, we were just grateful for everything?"

UNKNOWN

Be thankful and grateful for all things!

Thoughts/Actions:

167

"To love without condition, to talk without intention, to give without reason and to care without expectation. This is the art of true relationship."

UNKNOWN

I approached a kid and asked: "What is Love?" The kid answered: "Hmm, Love is when a puppy licks your face." I laughed, but then he added, "Even after you left him alone all day."

UNKNOWN

We too, can love, regardless.
"If in doubt, love."

UNKNOWN

168

"If you don't like where you are, then change it..... you are not a tree."

UNKNOWN

"If you don't like the news, go out and make some of your own."

WES NISKER

Thoughts/Actions:

169

"Mindset" {noun} a set of beliefs or a way of thinking that determines one's behavior, outlook and mental attitude.

UNKNOWN

A positive mindset doesn't cost anything, but is worth so much.

Thoughts/Actions:

170

"So why is a car's windshield so large and the rear view mirror so small? Because our past is not as important as our future. So, look ahead and move on."

UNKNOWN

Thoughts/Actions:

171

The ABC's of Genuine Happiness:

Accept your reality.
Be present. Be bold.
Create something exciting.
Drink plenty of water. Dance.
Exercise daily. Eat fresh foods.
Feel your emotions. Face fear.
Go outside and observe nature. Give.
Hug often. Help others.
Ignite your passions.
Jump through your comfort zone.
Kiss passionately.
Keep looking forward.
Laugh. Love. Learn to let go.
Meditate daily. Make goals.
Never give up on what you want.
Own a pet. Observe beauty.
Pray. Paint. Play an instrument.
Quit a bad habit. Quiet your mind.

Read. Relax. Reinvent yourself.
Smile. Sleep. Simplify.

Take power naps. Talk wisely.
Unleash your strengths.
Vent. Visualize your dreams.
Walk. Write. Watch the sun set.
Xerox your smiling face.
Yell less. Yield to your thoughts.
Zap negativity.

UNKNOWN

Thoughts/Actions:

172

"I shiver, thinking how easy it is to be totally wrong about people-to see one tiny part of them and confuse it for the whole, to see the cause and think it's the effect or vice versa."

LAUREN OLIVER

Thoughts/Actions:

173

"The secret to encouraging others is to get excited about the right things. Some people get excited about pointing out mistakes or finding someone's failures. Instead we should get excited about their strengths and the little things they're doing right."

JOHN C. MAXWELL

Get excited and focus on YOUR strengths and the little things you do right as well.

Thoughts/Actions:

174

"We are all born ignorant, but one must work hard to remain stupid."

BENJAMIN FRANKLIN

Here's to growing ourselves.

Thoughts/Actions:

175

From a dog to its beloved owner:

"My Face may be white, but my heart is pure gold. There is no shame in growing old."

FUNNYPAWS.COM

There's no shame in growing older.... it just means that your heart has had more time to experience & express LOVE.

"Everything on this planet is in a constant state of change, continuously growing, adapting, evolving. Actually, everything in this galaxy. You are not an exception. Embrace change. You are not here to stay idle and stagnant."

Thoughts/Actions:

176

"Choose to be optimistic, it feels better."

DALAI LAMA

"Optimism is the faith that leads to achievement. Nothing can be done without hope and confidence."

HELEN KELLER

Your brain without optimism...
Ho- hum
Your brain on optimism.... YEAH! Limitless

Have fun with this! Become aware, and choose to feel better... it's always YOUR choice! Choose to be optimistic and have a blast doing so!

Thoughts/Actions:

177

"When life is sweet, say thank you
and celebrate. And when life is
bitter, say thank you and grow."

UNKNOWN

Thoughts/Actions:

178

What can you do right now to turn
your life around?? Gratitude.

Thoughts/Actions:

179

"I've learned that everyone wants to live on top of
the mountain, but all the happiness and growth
occurs while you're climbing it."

UNKNOWN

Enjoy the climb.

Thoughts/Actions:

180

~~Good things come to those who wait.~~
No.
Good things come to those who work
their butts off and never give up.

UNKNOWN

Take action & follow your dreams.

Thoughts/Actions:

181

7 Lovely Logics

UNKNOWN

1. Make peace with your past so it doesn't spoil your present.

2. What others think about you is none of your business.

3. Time heals almost everything; give the time, some time.

4. Don't compare your life with other's you have no idea what their journey is all about.

5. No one is a reason of your happiness except yourself.

6. Stop thinking too much it's alright not to know all the answers.

7. Smile, you don't own all the problems of world.

Thoughts/Actions:

182

"Every person from your past lives as a shadow in your mind. Good or bad, they all helped you write the story of your life, and shaped the person you are today."

DOE ZANTAMATA

Thoughts/Actions:

183

"Learn everything you can, anytime you can, from anyone you can. You will be grateful you did."

UNKNOWN

Finding a Holy Man

Word spread across the countryside about the wise Holy Man who lived in a small house atop the mountain. A man from the village decided to make the long and difficult journey to visit him.

When he arrived at the house, he saw an old servant inside who greeted him at the door.

"I would like to see the wise Holy Man," he said to the servant.

The servant smiled and led him inside. As they walked through the house, the man from the village looked eagerly around the house, anticipating his encounter with the Holy Man.

Before he knew it, he had been led to the back door and escorted outside. He stopped and turned to the servant,

"But I want to see the Holy Man!"

"You already have," said the old man. "Everyone you may meet in life, even if they appear plain and insignificant... see each of them as a wise Holy Man. If you do this, then whatever problem you brought here today will be solved."

ZEN STORY

Thoughts/Actions:

184

"Your mind is a garden; your thoughts
are the seeds. You can grow flowers
or you can grow weeds."

UNKNOWN

Be aware of what you are thinking about today, because it truly makes a difference. When you catch yourself "growing weeds" with negative thoughts, immediately replace them with positive ones–thoughts that make you smile or bring you joy. Do this enough, and it will become an amazing habit. And have fun with it. That's really the whole point!

Thoughts/Actions:

185

"When a train goes through a tunnel and it gets dark, you don't throw away the ticket and jump off. You sit still and trust the engineer."

CORRIE TEN BOOM

Hold on and have faith.

Thoughts/Actions:

186

"Worrying = Using your imagination to
create something you don't want."

UNKNOWN

Have a worry free day today. Try not to waste a
minute of your day worrying by trusting that it
will all work out. Use your imagination for better
things and have fun with it!

Thoughts/Actions:

187

"It is not happy people who are thankful.
It is thankful people who are happy."

UNKNOWN

Be thankful for the simple, every
day joys. By being truly thankful,
you can't help but be happy.

Thoughts/Actions:

188

"If you are going to doubt
something, doubt your limits."

DON WARD

Thoughts/Actions:

189

"Today what did I do for my mind?
My body? My spirit? My relationships?
My creativity and passion?"

UNKNOWN

It's all about balance. Try to take a few minutes
each day to focus on and nourish the things
that are most important for YOU, including
your relationships, health, and happiness. A few
minutes a day is all it takes.

Thoughts/Actions:

190

"When you truly Love your Self,
You will always choose Peace."

UNKNOWN

"Let the power of our self-love be strong enough
to break all the lies we were programmed to

believe—all the lies that tell us we are not good enough, or strong enough, or intelligent enough, that we cannot make it. Let the power of our self-love be so strong that we no longer need to live our life according to other people's opinions."~Unknown

Thoughts/Actions:

191

"The best day of your life is the one on which you decide your life is your own. No apologies or excuses. No one to lean on, rely on, or blame. The gift is yours–it is an amazing journey–and you alone are responsible for the quality of it. This is the day your life really begins."

BOB MOAWAD

It's so easy to make excuses and blame others. Only when we take full responsibility for our lives can we learn and become aware that we do indeed have a choice! If you find yourself feeling down and start to blame others, stop and realize it's your life and only you can decide how it's going to go. Once you've taken responsibility for that decision, you will be free and every day will be the best!

Thoughts/Actions:

192

"The tighter you squeeze, the less you have."

ZEN PROVERB

Thoughts/Actions:

193

"There are moments when our lives seem to be going in circles. Each time around if you are paying attention you can see something different and learn something new. It isn't always where you are that matters. Sometimes it is where you are looking and what you are looking for that matters. You decide how you see your life. Look for the beauty of it always."

A DIFFERENT APPROACH

Thoughts/Actions:

194

"If three of us travel together, I
shall find two teachers."

CONFUCIUS

See the teacher in everyone
you cross paths with...

Thoughts/Actions:

195

"You have brains in your head. You have feet in
your shoes. You can steer yourself in any direction
you choose. You're on your own. And you know
what you know. You are the guy who'll decide
where to go."

DR. SEUSS

Be sure you are steering yourself in
the direction you want to go.

Thoughts/Actions:

196

"Happiness is not something readymade.
It comes from your own actions."

DALAI LAMA

Thoughts/Actions:

197

"The story of your life will be written with or
without your help. The next chapter is happening
while you read this. Will you wait to see what it
says later, or will you help write it?"

UNKNOWN

Thoughts/Actions:

198

"At any given moment you have the power to
say: This is NOT how the story is going to end."

UNKNOWN

Thoughts/Actions:

199

Ghandi's 7 Dangers to Human Virtue

1. Wealth without work.

2. Pleasure without conscience.

3. Knowledge without character.

4. Business without ethics.

5. Science without humanity.

6. Religion without sacrifice.

7. Politics without principle.

Thoughts/Actions:

200

"Holding on to anger is like grasping a hot coal with the intent of throwing it at someone else; you are the one who gets burned."

BUDDHA

"There never was a good war or a bad peace."

BENJAMIN FRANKLIN

"An Eye for an Eye Will Make the Whole World Blind."

MOHANDAS GANDHI

Think about this, and move towards peace throughout your day and life. Don't be blinded by resentment. When you find yourself not understanding why someone did or said something hurtful, the most freeing thing to do is accept that you never will and just let it go. As the saying goes; "Let go or be dragged." Free yourself from any resentment that you have by focusing only on becoming the person you want to be. By doing this, any resentment or negative feelings you have will simply fall away.

Thoughts/Actions:

201

Love is the solution to everything.

I love simplicity because I think at times we tend to make things more difficult than they need to be. There is one solution to all that is negative, and that is LOVE. Let's focus on the solution. And here's a reminder of what LOVE really is:

Love is patient, love is kind and is not jealous; love does not brag and is not arrogant. It does not envy, it does not boast, it is not proud. It is not rude; it does not act unbecomingly; it is not self-seeking, it is not easily angered, it keeps no record of wrongs. Love does not delight in evil but rejoices with the truth. It always protects, always trusts, always hopes, always perseveres.

1 CORINTHIANS 13

Thoughts/Actions:

202

"Be not afraid of growing slowly; be afraid only of standing still."

CHINESE PROVERB

"It doesn't matter how slow you go, as long as you don't stop..."

UNKNOWN

"I may not be there yet, but I'm closer than I was yesterday."

UNKNOWN

Keep moving in the right direction and have a great day!

Thoughts/Actions:

203

"My friends, LOVE is better than
anger. HOPE is better than fear.
OPTIMISM is better than despair."

JACK LAYTON

Thoughts/Actions:

204

"Believe it or not, you are in control of your own
life. You are the reason why you're sad, and you're
the reason why you're happy. Don't let anyone else
tell you otherwise. So, don't wait for happiness.
Go out and find it. Right now. And don't let anyone
else tell you otherwise."

UNKNOWN

Thoughts/Actions:

205

"An invisible thread connects those who are
destined to meet, regardless of time, place, or
circumstance. The thread may stretch or tangle,
but it will never break. May you be open to each
thread that comes into your life–the golden ones

and the coarse ones—and may you weave them
into a brilliant and beautiful life."

UNKNOWN

"ONE BIG UNIVERSE. And I had
the privilege to meet YOU."

UNKNOWN

Thoughts/Actions:

206

"Be silly. Be Honest. Be kind."

RALPH WALDO EMERSON

Easy recipe for an awesome life!

Thoughts/Actions:

207

"If you end up with a boring miserable life because
you listened to your mom, your dad, your teacher,
your priest, or some guy on television telling you
how to do your shit, then you deserve it."

FRANK ZAPPA

Be true to yourself and live an authentic life.

Thoughts/Actions:

208

"This is a new day. Begin anew to
claim and create all that is good."

LOUISE HAY

Don't get stuck in the past or worry about the
future. Every day is a new day, and you get to
create it!

Thoughts/Actions:

209

"Let NO ONE be the writer of
YOUR life story. The End."

UNKNOWN

Thoughts/Actions:

210

"We enjoy warmth because we have been cold.
We appreciate light because we have been in
darkness. By the same token, we can experience
joy because we have known sadness."

UNKNOWN

Thoughts/Actions:

211

"We're not perfect. Any of us. We
screw up. We make mistakes. But then
we forgive and move forward."

UNKNOWN

Accept that we are all human and will make
mistakes. Then forgive yourself and others and
move forward.

Thoughts/Actions:

212

1. Find what makes you happy.
2. Do it.

UNKNOWN

Thoughts/Actions:

213

"Happiness is native to the human mind and
its physical machine. We think better, perform
better, feel better, and are healthier when we are
happy."

MAXWELL MALTZ

Thoughts/Actions:

214

"No one is born with hatred or intolerance."

UNKNOWN

"No one is born hating another person because of the color of his skin, or his background, or his religion. People must learn to hate, and if they can learn to hate, they can be taught to love, for love comes naturally to the human heart."

NELSON MANDELA

Let's find our way back to the loving, accepting creatures that we were born to be.

Thoughts/Actions:

215

"Whenever you're making an important decision, ask yourself first if it gets you closer to your goals or farther away. If the answer is closer, pull the trigger. If it's farther away, make a different choice. Conscious choice-making is a critical step in making your dreams a reality."

JILLIAN MICHAELS

Thoughts/Actions:

216

"Just imagine how much you'd get done if you stopped actively sabotaging your own work."

SETH GODIN

You work so hard to not let
your teachers and peers down.
You work so hard to not let
your boss and co-workers down.
You work so hard to not let
your friends and family down.
But more importantly, don't let
YOURSELF down.

Thoughts/Actions:

217

"The purpose of our lives is to be happy."

DALAI LAMA

Do things to make yourself happy
today. That's your purpose!

Thoughts/Actions:

218

"The best way to get even is to forget."

UNKNOWN

Here's to a new day!

Thoughts/Actions:

219

12 Symptoms of a Spiritual Awakening

1. An increased tendency to let things happen rather than make them happen.

2. Frequent attacks of smiling.

3. Feelings of being connected with others and nature.

4. Frequent overwhelming episodes of appreciation.

5. A tendency to think and act spontaneously rather than from fears based on past experience.

6. An unmistakable ability to enjoy each moment.

7. A loss of ability to worry.

8. A loss of interest in conflict.

9. A loss of interest in interpreting the actions of others.

10. A loss of interest in judging others.

11. A loss of interest in judging self.

12. Gaining the ability to love without expecting anything in return.

Thoughts/Actions:

220

"When you live on a round planet,
there's no choosing sides."

Dr. Wayne Dyer

Thoughts/Actions:

221

"Remember this, that very little is
needed to make a happy life."

MARCUS AURELIUS

Thoughts/Actions:

222

"Your life is a book; Don't jump to the end to see
if it's worth it. Just enjoy life And fill make those
pages with
Beautiful memories."

UNKNOWN

Thoughts/Actions:

223

"Whether you pushed me or pulled me, drained me or fueled me, loved me or left me, hurt me or helped me, you are part of my growth and no kidding, I thank you."

UNKNOWN

Be thankful for all of it...

Thoughts/Actions:

224

"Very first thing I do when I get lost driving... Turn down the radio."

UNKNOWN

Does anyone else do this too? I think it's interesting that becoming quiet when lost is instinctual, and helps people find their way.

Thoughts/Actions:

225

"The voice in your head that says
that you can't do this is a liar."

UNKNOWN

You have two voices within you that you listen to all day long. It's important to know the difference between the two. One is sometimes referred to as the "ego self" while the other as the "true self". The ego self or mind is a tool and although you shouldn't fight it, you should be aware of it and realize that it is based on physical perspective and false concepts. It has been created by outside sources and opinions, based on judgments, envy, greed, jealousy, etc. The "true self" speaks the underlying truth, is based on love, and always brings about a sense of peace and contentment. The "true self" will not fight the "ego self", therefore, the negative voice often overpowers the true voice within. Listening to both voices will cause confusion and chaos; therefore, it's up to you. Practice silencing the negative voice and remember it's lying to you, and then peace and contentment and all that is good will be yours.

Thoughts/Actions:

226

How to save your heart?

SHOULD:
Never expect.
Never demand.
Never assume.

KNOW:
Your limits.
Where you stand.
Your role.

DONT:
Get affected.
Get jealous.
Get paranoid.

JUST:
Be contented.
Go with the flow
And stay happy.

Sounds easy right? With practice it can be.

Thoughts/Actions:

227

"Unless someone like you cares a whole awful lot, nothing is going to get better. It's not."

DR. SEUSS, THE LORAX

Thoughts/Actions:

228

"The past cannot be change, forgotten, edited, or erased. It can only be accepted."

UNKNOWN

Have an accepting day!

Thoughts/Actions:

229

"Never Fear shadows. They simply mean there's a light shining somewhere nearby."

RUTH E. RENKEL

Thoughts/Actions:

230

"What activities would be worth your
precious time and attention today?"

UNKNOWN

Thoughts/Actions:

231

"Stop competing with others. Start
competing with yourself."

UNKNOWN

Thoughts/Actions:

232

"Experience is the name everyone
gives to mistakes."

UNKNOWN

Thoughts/Actions:

233

"If you are depressed, you are living in the past.

If you are anxious, you are living in the future.

If you are at peace,
you are living in the present."

LAO TZU

Here's to living in the now!

Thoughts/Actions:

234

"Everything you've ever done, every person
you've ever met, every experience you've ever had
is a part of who you are today, adding interesting
layers to your being and colorful depths to your
soul."

KAREN SALMANSOHN

Here's to appreciating all of it
as we continue to grow.

Thoughts/Actions:

235

"People take different roads seeking fulfillment
and happiness. Just because they're not on
your road doesn't mean they've gotten lost."

DALAI LAMA

Thoughts/Actions:

236

"Never argue with stupid people. They
will drag you down to their level and
then beat you with experience."

MARK TWAIN

Thoughts/Actions:

237

"If you want to feel rich...
Just count all of the things you
have that money cannot buy."

UKNOWN

Always take time to count your blessings.

#1. You're breathing

#2. You have eyes to see this, along with all the beauty that nature naturally provides.

Keep going!

Thoughts/Actions:

238

Do what you LOVE. LOVE what you do."

UNKNOWN

Thoughts/Actions:

239

"Today what did I do for
My mind?
My body?
My spirit?
My relationships?
My creativity and Passion?"

UNKNOWN

Thoughts/Actions:

240

"Waiting for someone else to make you happy is the best way to be sad."

UNKNOWN

Make yourself happy....
because you can! :)
And have a fantastic day!

Thoughts/Actions:

241

"Somedays you just have to create your own sunshine."

UNKNOWN

Create your own sunshine today.... because YOU can!

Thoughts/Actions:

242

Some people see the glass half full. Others see it half empty. Some people grumble that roses have thorns; some are grateful that thorns have roses.

"The difference between a mountain
and a molehill is your perspective."

AL NEUHARTH

Thoughts/Actions:

243

Remember how BIG our
Universe is.

If you have a problem, try not to focus all of your attention on it. People tend to lose focus and sometimes turn little problems into big problems. Try to step back and look at the bigger picture. The purpose is not to ignore or minimize how serious your problem is, but to gain a new and different perspective. Some people call this "being the witness". Visualize yourself looking down at your situation from the ceiling. Then visualize your situation from an airplane, then from the moon where you can see the entire Earth, etc.

Live, laugh, love, and focus on
things that bring you joy!

Thoughts/Actions:

244

"The best things in life are free.
Hugs
Smiles
Friends
Kisses
Family
Sleep
Love
Laughter
Good memories"

UNKNOWN

Thoughts/Actions:

245

Forgiveness

"Anyone can hold a grudge, but it takes a person with character to forgive. When you forgive, you release yourself from a painful burden. Forgiveness doesn't mean what happened was OK, and it doesn't mean that person should still be welcome in your life. It just means you have made peace with the pain and are ready to let it go."

UNKNOWN

When you forgive, you release
yourself from a painful burden.

Thoughts/Actions:

246

How to Save Your Own Life

1. Renounce useless guilt.

2. Don't make a cult of suffering.

3. Live in the Now (or at least the Soon).

4. Always do the things you fear the most; courage is an acquired taste, like a caviar.

5. Trust all joy.

6. If the evil eye fixes you in its gaze, look elsewhere.

7. Get ready to be eighty-seven.

FROM THE NOVEL HOW TO SAVE YOUR OWN LIFE,
BY ERICA JONG

Thoughts/Actions:

247

"The real test in life is not in keeping out of the rough, but in getting out after you are in."

UNKNOWN

Thoughts/Actions:

248

"If we all did things we are capable of doing, we would literally astound ourselves."

THOMAS EDISON

Thoughts/Actions:

249

"I beg young people to travel. If you don't have a passport, get one. Take a summer, get a backpack and go to Delhi, go to Saigon, go to Bangkok, go to Kenya. Have your mind blown. Eat interesting food. Dig some interesting people. Have an adventure. Be careful. Come back and you're going to see your country differently, you're going to see your president differently, no matter who it is. Music, culture, food, water. Your showers will become shorter. You're going to get a sense of what globalization looks like. It's not what Tom Friedman writes about; I'm sorry. You're going to see that global climate change is very real. And that for some people, their day consists of walking 12 miles for four buckets of water. And so there are lessons that you can't get out of a book that are waiting for you at the other end of that flight. A lot of people—Americans and Europeans—come back and go, Ohhhhh. And the light bulb goes on."

HENRY ROLLINS

Just knowing "that for some people, their day consists of walking 12 miles for four buckets of water" can help put things into perspective. Or that every time you sit down to eat, there are millions of people out there who haven't eaten in days. It can help us appreciate the things that we take for granted and inspire us to reach out and help others in need. Let's open our eyes and look at things differently.

Thoughts/Actions:

250

YOUR LIFE

"It's time to take your life back from the people that are causing you pain and making you unhappy. Remember, this is your LIFE and you

are the author of your story. If you're stuck on the
same page... just remember that at any moment
you have the power to write a new chapter."

UNKNOWN

Thoughts/Actions:

251

"There are two ways to be fooled. One
is to believe what isn't true; the other
is to refuse to accept what is true."

SOREN KIERKEGAARD

Here's to opening our eyes to the truth.

Thoughts/Actions:

252

"The consequences of today are determined by
the actions of the past. To change your future,
alter your decisions today."

Unknown

Thoughts/Actions:

253

"A good choice today... will lead
to a better tomorrow...

We have the power to choose... Use it wisely..."

UNKNOWN

"The statement "I have no choice" is a lie. Be
honest with yourself as to why you are choosing
to do a particular thing. Then, do it gladly,
knowing that you are always getting to do what
you want. You can choose. Isn't that power?"

NEALE DONALD WALSCH

Thoughts/Actions:

254

"Negativity is TOXIC. Protect
yourself! With positivity."

UNKNOWN

When you find yourself being confronted
with negativity, change the subject or simply
walk away. Being positive is good for your
soul, your health, your sanity, and your life!

Thoughts/Actions:

255

Never waste your time wondering about what might have been. Get busy thinking about what still might be, trusting that whatever it is, it will leave you glad that what might have been never came to be.

SANDRA KING

"And there's no such thing as what might have been. That's a waste of time. Drive you out of your mind"

TIM MCGRAW, RED RAGTOP

Thoughts/Actions:

256

"Whatever your excuse is, it is time to stop believing it."

UNKNOWN

Thoughts/Actions:

257

"The tiny SEED knew that in order to GROW
it needed to be dropped in DIRT, covered in
darkness, and STRUGGLE to reach the LIGHT."

UNKNOWN

Thoughts/Actions:

258

"When anything happens in life, there's a 3-step
approach to handling it:

1. It is what it is; accept it. It will either control
   you or you can control it. (You can only
   control how YOU handle a situation. You can
   be in control with acceptance, not resistance.
   When you resist what is, you prolong your
   own suffering. What you resist, persists.
   With acceptance you free yourself to move
   forward.)

2. Harvest the good; there's good in
   everything.

3. Forgive all the rest."

DR. MICHAEL BERNARD BECKWITH

Thoughts/Actions:

259

"I want to remember that I am not my title, my position, my possessions, my appearance, my neighborhood, my age, my body size, my race or my income level... I am a soul."

UNKNOWN

Thoughts/Actions:

260

"Everything is energy and that's all there is to it. Match the frequency of the reality you want and you cannot help but get that reality. It can be no other way. This is not philosophy. This is physics."

DARRYL ANKA

We are energy. Energy can be measured by frequencies or vibrations. The higher your frequency, the happier, joyful, and peaceful you will be. The lower your frequency, the more depressed, sad, and miserable you will be. You can raise your vibration with intention. Simple things known to raise vibration:

Singing, dancing
Laughing
Spending time with cheerful, positive people

Being positive,
finding the good in everything
Spending time in nature,
connecting with your higher self
Eating healthy foods and
living a healthy lifestyle
Exercising, meditating,
yoga on a regular basis
Loving one another

Start today. Go ahead, start singing! Raise your vibration to a higher frequency, and you will start attracting things, people, and possibilities that match it. It's the law of the Universe.

Thoughts/Actions:

261

"Don't ever let someone tell you that you can't do something. Not even me. You got a dream, you gotta protect it. When people can't do something themselves, they're gonna tell you that you can't do it. If you want something, go get it. Period."

WILL SMITH THE PURSUIT OF HAPPYNESS

Thoughts/Actions:

262

"You can't always be nice. That's how people take advantage of you. Sometimes you have to set boundaries."

UNKNOWN

Thoughts/Actions:

263

20 Things to Start Doing

1. Drink a lot of water and/or green tea.
2. Eat a big breakfast, average lunch, tiny dinner.
3. Eat fruit, vegetable, and natural foods.
4. Go for a walk/swim/bike ride.
5. Read a book.
6. Go to bed earlier.
7. Stop thinking negative thoughts about yourself or others.
8. Don't dwell on the past–turn it into art.
9. Enjoy the little things in life.
10. Do not judge or compare yourself to others.
11. Begin yoga or meditation.
12. Do not put things off.
13. Avoid processed food.
14. Stretch daily to increase flexibility.
15. Listen to peaceful music.

16. Live in a tidy space.
17. Wear clothes that make you happy.
18. Throw away things you don't need.
19. Remember that all the effort you are making now will pay off in the end.
20. Go outside more.

20 Things to Start Doing. Don't just read them. Start implementing them today. Can you do at least half of these and add more with each new day? Write them down and check off when completed for an amazing life full of joy and peace.

Thoughts/Actions:

264

"Being nice to someone you dislike doesn't mean you're a fake. It means you are mature enough to tolerate your dislike towards them."

UNKNOWN

Thoughts/Actions:

265

"Be open to all the good coming your way."

UNKNOWN

Thoughts/Actions:

266

"Real knowledge is to know the
extent of one's own ignorance."

CONFUCIUS

Thoughts/Actions:

267

"When I was young, I admired clever people.
Now that I am old, I admire kind people."

ABRAHAM JOSHUA HESCHEL

Thoughts/Actions:

268

"Never explain yourself to anyone. Because
the person who likes you doesn't need it, and
the person who dislikes you won't believe it."

UNKNOWN

269

"There's so much grace in acceptance. It's not an easy concept, but if you embrace it, you'll find more peace than you ever imagined."

LORETTA LAROCHE

"The best way to escape from the past is not to avoid or forget it, but to accept and forgive it."

UNKNOWN

Thoughts/Actions:

270

Life Is Too Short

Laugh when you can
Apologize when you should
Let go of what you can't change
Learn from your mistake
Love deeply and forgive quickly!"

UNKNOWN

It doesn't have to be difficult. Do these few things and your life will be peaceful and full of JOY!

Thoughts/Actions:

271

"Ask more of yourself."

UNKNOWN

Thoughts/Actions:

272

"An arrow can only be shot by pulling it backward. When life is dragging you back with difficulties, just imagine that it's going to launch you into something great."

UNKNOWN

Thoughts/Actions:

273

"How would your life be different if...You stopped allowing other people to dilute or poison your day with their words or opinions? Let today be the day...You stand strong in the truth of your beauty and journey through your day without attachment to the validation of others"

STEVE MARABOLI

"Do not have an opinion while you listen because frankly, your opinion doesn't hold much water outside of Your Universe. Just listen. Listen until their brain has been twisted like a dripping towel and what they have to say is all over the floor."

HUGH ELLIOT

"Nothing is more conductive to peace of mind than not having any opinions at all."

GEORG CHRISTOPH LICHTENBERG

Thoughts/Actions:

274

Before you Talk, Listen.
Before you React, Think.
Before you Criticize, Wait.
Before you Pray, Forgive.
Before you Quit. Try.

UNKNOWN

Thoughts/Actions:

275

"Give yourself permission to close the door to toxic people in your life."

UNKNOWN

"You have the right to quit Toxic People. (They're contagious.)"

DR. SUNWOLF

When you finally decide to quit toxic people, it's not giving up. It's realizing your self-worth and that you no longer need certain people and the pain and frustration they cause in your life. Some people and relationships constantly drain your energy, in both obvious and subtle ways. We always hear about the ill effects that are caused by toxic foods or chemicals. Toxic people are just as unhealthy for us. Toxic people can drain you; physically, mentally and emotionally.

I don't think that toxic people intentionally try to drain or hurt others, and like everyone, they deserve love and respect. It's about becoming aware of how YOU feel when dealing with a certain person or relationship, and then making the necessary changes that will best benefit your well being.

If you're constantly feeling drained by a certain person or relationship, you need to make the changes necessary to rid yourself of that toxicity, because you're worth it!

Thoughts/Actions:

276

"You are not what other people think about you. You are whatever you decide to be!"

UNKNOWN

Decide to be kind, loving and forgiving; not only to others but to yourself as well. And then expect miracles to unfold in your life.

Thoughts/Actions:

277

"I fall, I rise, I make mistakes, I live. I've been hurt but I am alive. I'm human, I am not perfect. But, I'm thankful. Through them, I learned to appreciate LIFE..."

UNKNOWN

Thoughts/Actions:

278

"Never depend on other people as the source of your happiness or for approval. Depend on YOU!"

UNKNOWN

Thoughts/Actions:

279

"Life is like crossing a set of monkey bars... You can choose to just hang there, but in order to move forward, you'll eventually have to let go."

UNKNOWN

Thoughts/Actions:

280

Life Is Far Too Short
To be sad.
To be mad.
To hold regret.
To look back.
To be depressed
To be unkind.
Be nice and do good
Every day is NEW"

UNKNOWN

281

"May you leave behind
the pain of YESTERDAY,
cherish the moments of TODAY, and
embrace the happiness of TOMORROW."

UNKNOWN

Thoughts/Actions:

282

"Throughout life people will make you mad, disrespect you and treat you bad. Let God deal with the things they do because hate in your heart will consume you too."

WILL SMITH

When people make you mad, disrespect you, and treat you bad, don't take it personal. Most of the time it has nothing to do with you, and everything to do with their own insecurities, and the beliefs they've been conditioned to believe since childhood. It's not about you so don't allow yourself to get upset. It's a known fact that feeling negative emotions affects YOUR body and YOUR health in negative ways. Why do that to yourself? Learn to breathe and let it go. It's not about you. Nobody is perfect and we are all doing the best that we can. Do your best to let negative feelings go.

Thoughts/Actions:

283

Reiki Principles:

Just for today...
I will not be angry
I will not worry
I will be grateful
I will do my work honestly
I will be kind to every living thing

"Living by these five principles will ultimately lead the practitioner to the right path and provide guidance when at the path. And aid the practitioner to promote peace and harmony."

DR. MIKAO USUI, THE FIVE PRINCIPLES OF REIKI

Thoughts/Actions:

284

"Sometimes I write down tasks after I've done them, just to get the satisfaction of crossing them off my list."

UNKNOWN

Ever done this? Here's to a productive week! Remember breaking up big projects/goals into little steps is the key to getting things done and making your dreams a reality. One step at a time. Or as Dr. Martin Luther King Jr. said: "You don't have to see the whole staircase, just take the first step."

Thoughts/Actions:

285

"Accept everything about yourself. I mean everything you are and that is the beginning and the end. No apologies, no regrets."

UNKNOWN

We've all been dealt these cards, and our job is to play with them, rather than to demand a new deal. And so it's just like the fact that I'm 5 foot 8 and I have brown eyes rather than blue, I'm not 6 foot 3. All of these I see as givens and these are the circumstances with which I have to live my life. Rather than trying to force myself to be seven inches taller than I am or to have different color eyes than I do have. "

PICO IYER

Thoughts/Actions:

286

A principal offered the following words from a judge who regularly deals with youth:

"Always we hear the cry from teenagers, 'what can we do, where can we go?'

"My answer is this: go home, mow the lawn, wash the windows, learn to cook, build a raft, get a job, visit the sick, study your lessons and after you've finished, read a book. Your town does not owe you recreational facilities and your parents do not owe you fun."

"The world does not owe you a living, you owe the world something. You owe it your time, energy and talent so that no one will be at war, in sickness and lonely again.

In other words grow up, stop being a cry baby, get out of your dream world and develop a backbone not a wishbone. Start behaving like a responsible person.

You are important and you are needed. It's too late to sit around and wait for somebody to do something someday. Someday is now and that somebody is you!"

Great advice for teens and adults alike! Let's do it!

Thoughts/Actions:

287

Coincident or Not?

If,

A B C D E F G H I J K L M N O
P Q R S T U V W X Y Z

Equals,

1 2 3 4 5 6 7 8 9 10 11 12 13 14 15 16
17 18 19 20 21 22 23 34 25 26

Then,

K+N+O+W+L+E+D+G+E
11+14+15+23+12+5+4+7+5=96%

H+A+R+D+W+O+R+K
8+1+18+4+23+15+18+11=98%

Both are important, but the total falls just short
of 100%

But,

A+T+T+I+T+U+D+E
1+20+20+9+20+21+4+5=100%

"The greatest discovery of all time is
that a person can change his future
by merely changing his attitude."

OPRAH WINFREY

Thoughts/Actions:

131

288

Remember this the next time you
get frustrated with someone.

"He that wrestles with us strengthens
our nerves, and sharpens our skill.
Our antagonist is our helper."

EDMUND BURKE

Thoughts/Actions:

289

"Don't take anything personally, even when
a situation seems so personal, even if others
insult you directly, it has nothing to do with
you. Their point of view and opinion come from
all the programming they received growing up.
Whatever people do, feel, think or say don't take
it personally. It's not about you, it's about them.
There is a huge amount of freedom that comes to
you when you take nothing personally."

DON MIGUEL RUIZ

Thoughts/Actions:

290

"Don't feel bad if people only remember you when they need you. Feel privileged that you are like a candle that comes to their minds when there is darkness."

UNKNOWN

I love this quote because it's taking something that most would get upset about and making it positive. You can either take it personal when it seems like someone only remembers you when they need you, or you can change the way you look at it. By taking it personal, you are only hurting yourself and possibly causing more pain.

Love doesn't keep score, but the ego does. The ego keeps constant score of what it believes to be injustices. The ego is resistance and argumentative, and we only get hurt or hurt others when we are coming from that place.

To the ego, power comes from getting; and to love, power comes from giving. Let's return to love. Let's look at things differently. Be aware of your thoughts and free yourself. Love doesn't compete, therefore, love never fails.

Thoughts/Actions:

291

"Before you judge someone...
walk a mile in his shoes!"

UNKNOWN

"Do you understand that if you were to live my life from day one that you would have made the same exact choices that I have made and done the same exact things that I have done?"

UNKNOWN

I think the above quote defines respect and compassion. I also think it's difficult for most to truly comprehend, yet for some reason it's so very easy to think that we would have done differently. Why is that I wonder???

Everyone is on their own journey. We need to trust and respect that everyone is learning and growing at the pace that is right for them, and in perfect time.

Thoughts/Actions:

292

"Start everyday with a new hope,
leave bad memories behind and have
faith for a better tomorrow."

UNKNOWN

Why do so many of us choose to stay stuck? We have the power to do this.... so will you do it? Will you start everyday with a new hope, leave bad memories behind and have faith for a better tomorrow?

Once you master this daily, work towards mastering it hourly. Start every hour with a new hope, leaving "bad" memories, experiences, and decisions behind, while having faith that every new hour will be better and bring you more peace, love, and joy. You don't have to wait for a new day. You can start wherever you are right NOW. Letting go of thoughts and things that no longer benefit you will allow and make room for new opportunities and unexpected blessings.

Thoughts/Actions:

293

"The reason we struggle with insecurity is because we compare our behind-the-scenes with everyone else's highlight reel."

STEVEN FURTICK

Be thankful for all of it. There is no benefit in comparing your life to other people's "highlight reel". Trust that everyone's journey is different for a reason. And keep in mind that some of the richest and wealthiest people are the most sad and miserable, while some of the poorest people (who have very little) are the most free and happy. Happiness is not external. Come from a place of gratitude, even for your "behind-the-scene" times, while trusting that all is as it should be. When you can truly do this, without feeling any sense of lack, amazing things will come into your life because your true thoughts and feelings attract more of the same. Remember you can't fight it because it's one of the laws of the Universe and you get to choose. So maybe I should say that internal happiness makes for external happiness.

Thoughts/Actions:

294

"Don't dwell on the wrong decisions you've made. Take the lesson and move forward. It's okay, just make sure you take the opportunity to do it right the next time."

UNKNOWN

This is great. Have you ever made a mistake? Or wished you would have said or done something differently? Don't dwell on it. Trust that you wouldn't have learned the lesson otherwise. Let it go and move forward with good intentions.

Thoughts/Actions:

295

"Talking about our problems
is our greatest addiction.
Break the habit. Talk about your joys."

RITA SCHIANO

Can YOU do it? Of course you can! Break the habit, and create a joyful life.

Thoughts/Actions:

296

"A person who is nice to YOU but is NOT
nice to the waiter IS NOT a nice person."

UNKNOWN

I waited tables for seven years, while in high school
and college. Thankfully I don't recall having to
deal with many mean or rude people. Most of my
days were filled with extremely kind, considerate,
and fun people. But I believe that a person who is
nice to YOU, but is rude to anyone else, is NOT a
nice person.

People (including waiters) make mistakes, and
we learn from them. But being rude doesn't
accomplish anything. I know people like to
justify their rudeness, but in reality they are
only hurting themselves more by lowering their
vibration. There's no benefit in being mean, rude,
or negative. Ever. Do you think?

Thoughts/Actions:

297

"There are no mistakes. The events we bring
upon ourselves, no matter how unpleasant, are
necessary in order to learn what we need to

learn; whatever steps we take, they're necessary to reach the places we've chosen to go."

RICHARD BACH

Imagine how freeing it would be if we could bring ourselves to believe this. Well now is the time. Believe it! Let yourself off the hook. We are all learning and growing. All is as it should be.

Thoughts/Actions:

298

"I Choose...
to live by choice, not by chance;
to make changes, not excuses;
to be motivated, not manipulated;
to be useful, not used;
to excel, not compete.
I choose self-esteem, not self pity.
I choose to listen to my inner voice,
not the random opinion of others."

UNKNOWN

Have a great day choosing wisely for yourself.

Thoughts/Actions:

299

"If I had a dollar for every time my dog
made me smile, I would be a millionaire."

UNKNOWN

"One reason a dog can be such a comfort when
you're feeling blue is that he doesn't try to find
out why. Dogs wag their tails, not their tongues."

UNKNOWN

"It is scarcely possible to doubt that the love
of man has become instinctive in the dog."

CHARLES DARWIN

Oh but the goal should be to love like dogs. Should
it be so hard? Showing unconditional love; being
forgiving, accepting, nonjudgmental, and living
joyously in the present moment without fail?

Thoughts/Actions:

300

"The body heals with play, the mind heals
with laughter, and the spirit heals with joy."

PROVERB

Thoughts/Actions:

301

"If you turn it over to the universe, you will be surprised and dazzled by what is delivered to you. This is where magic and miracles happen."

JOE VITALE

"Believe that you can and you are HALF WAY there."

UNKNOWN

Doubt is just a thought. And believe it or not, YOU are in control of your thoughts. Put the doubts aside and start believing! Always replace doubtful thoughts with unquestionable faith, and amazing things will start to happen. Just be aware, doubt will want to creep back in. But each time you replace your negative thoughts it will become easier and easier to believe. Believe that you can and you're half way there. Once you truly believe, the Universe will work with you to make your dreams/goals a reality, and it will be effortless.

Thoughts/Actions:

302

"Imagine a world where people line up to help their fellow man, like they line up to buy the newest iphone."

UNKNOWN

Can you imagine? I can! Let's line up to help one another. And remember, you get what you give.

"It is literally true that you can succeed best and quickest by helping others to succeed."

NAPOLEON HILL

Thoughts/Actions:

303

:(:
Happy or Sad
You decide.

Thoughts/Actions:

304

"Choose Inner Peace. Nothing is worth losing your inner peace. Take action as circumstances require, but never surrender your inner peace. Stop. Breathe deeply. Close your eyes and breathe deeply again. Then, and only then, take action from a peaceful heart."

JONATHAN LOCKWOOD HUIE

"Inner peace begins the moment you choose not to allow another person or event to control your emotions!"

UNKNOWN

Here's to inner peace.

Thoughts/Actions:

305

"By letting it go, it all gets done. The world is won by those who let it go. But when you try and try. The world is beyond the winning."

LAO TZU

Thoughts/Actions:

306

"When guilt runs your life, you are living in the past. When worry fills your mind, you live in the future. Keep your head where your feet are, and you will live with peace."

LISA VILLA PROSEN

Practice enjoying THIS moment without looking back or worrying about tomorrow.

Thoughts/Actions:

307

"Arguing with a fool only proves
that there are TWO."

UNKNOWN

Thoughts/Actions:

308

"Whatever is going on in your mind
IS what you are attracting."

UNKNOWN

The Law of Attraction has always fascinated me. The fact that you WILL attract whatever it is you are thinking about or focusing on, even if it's clearly something you don't want and not in your best interest. So you may know that something is not in your best interest, but if you can't control your thoughts, unfortunately you will attract it to you–eventually there it will be, staring you in the face. Hence the saying, "Thoughts become things".

Are your thoughts full of lack and worry or of abundance and gratitude? The Law of Attraction works in both positive and negative ways and you get to choose.

I picture people playing with the Law of Gravity when it was first discovered, and learning from it. With the Law of Gravity we learned that jumping off a building can lead to devastating results; therefore, we don't do it. So let's play with the Law of Attraction. Have fun with it. Control your thoughts. When you find yourself thinking something that you know does not benefit you, immediately change the thought to something incredibly positive. Visualize yourself someplace you know you'd like to be or driving your dream car, etc., etc.; as long as you change your thought pattern. I know it can be challenging, but only when you truly become aware of your thoughts, can you master it. Once you have your thoughts under control, then you can just sit back and watch miracles happen.

Thoughts/Actions:

309

"Someday everything will make perfect sense. So, for now, laugh at the confusion, smile through the tears and keep reminding yourself that everything happens for a reason."

UNKNOWN

Stop over-thinking it. Over-thinking causes unnecessary stress and worry, and tends to blow things out of proportion. Go with the flow and enjoy the ride trusting that if it's meant to be it will be.

310

"The expert in anything was once a beginner."

UNKNOWN

What do you want to do? What are your dreams? Big or small, get started now because the expert in anything was once a beginner.

"My father used to say that it's never too late to do anything you wanted to do. And he said, 'You never know what you can accomplish until you try."

MICHAEL JORDAN

Thoughts/Actions:

311

"No one is perfect, that's why pencils have erasers."

UNKNOWN

"I have not failed. I've just found 10,000 ways that won't work."

THOMAS A. EDISON

Be proud of your "failures", recognizing that they are not failures if you've learned from them.

312

"Do not let the behavior of others
destroy your inner peace."

UNKNOWN

"A battle against anything is a battle against
you... and your alignment with source."

UNKNOWN

This really isn't difficult to comprehend. A battle of any kind is a battle against you. So knowing this, wouldn't it make perfect sense to end all battles and arguments; or at least not become willing participants of them? It's okay if someone disagrees with you–because people have a right to their opinions–but have enough respect to let it end there. If someone has said or done something you disagree with, it's okay to distance yourself from that, which does not feel good, but live and let live while trusting that each person is on their own path. If something doesn't feel right and you feel the need, voice your opinion respectfully, and then let it go. Don't allow differences of opinions to create conflict because then you cause inner conflict within yourself which doesn't make any sense at all.

A battle against anything is a battle against you, so let's be smart and put an end to the things that do not benefit us. Ending all battles allows for inner peace to flow. And inner peace and serenity are good for your health, and feel good too!

Thoughts/Actions:

313

"Men often hate each other because they fear each other; they fear each other because they don't know each other; they don't know each other because they can not communicate; they cannot communicate because they are separated."

MARTIN LUTHER KING JR.

"We must learn to live together as brothers or perish together as fools."

DR. MARTIN LUTHER KING, JR.

Here's to unity and love, and to realizing we are all the same... human.

Thoughts/Actions:

314

"One Of The Simplest Ways To Stay Happy; Just
Let Go Of The Things That Make You Sad..."

UNKNOWN

"Don't carry your mistakes around with you.
Instead, place them under your feet and use
them as stepping stones to rise above them!"

UNKNOWN

Thoughts/Actions:

315

"If you have nothing to be grateful
for, check your pulse."

UNKNOWN

"There shall be eternal summer
in the grateful heart."

CELIA THAXTER

"Let's choose today to quench our thirst for the
'good life' we think others lead by acknowledging
the good that already exists in our lives. We can
then offer the universe the gift of our grateful
hearts."

SARAH BAN BREATHNACH

Thoughts/Actions:

316

"Your words carry amazing power. So when you speak
make sure you uplift someone
and never put them down."

UNKNOWN

Words are powerful. Use yours to uplift and encourage. And remember what you give out you get back. Have a wonderful day!

Thoughts/Actions:

317

"Things always have a way of working out."

UNKNOWN

How awesome is this?! Things always work out! It's too bad we couldn't trust this during difficult times. We would save ourselves a lot of unnecessary suffering. It happens and you see it all the time. How often do we think we are at our lowest and that the pain will never end, only to get on the other side of it, and realize that life is so much better? There are so many instances where people experience difficult situations: breakups/divorces, the loss of jobs, extreme debt, the list goes on and on; some kind of change that is upsetting because it wasn't in the plan or expected. But once the pain passes, and we move forward, we look back and can't even imagine going back to the way it was before because the change has been so surprisingly wonderful. And we have learned and grown, and life has given us so many amazing new experiences that we would have totally missed out on.

When you're feeling down, hold your head high and stay strong. Trust that things always work out and that on the other side of the discomfort, something far better is waiting for you! And then, enjoy!

Thoughts/Actions:

318

Self Discipline

Some say the secret to success in all areas is self-discipline. Self-discipline to eat right, to exercise, to spend quality time with your family, to get your work done, to relax, to go to bed on time, to avoid negative people and negativity in general, to control your thoughts, to do the right thing, etc.

"Respect your efforts, respect yourself. Self-respect leads to self-discipline. When you have both firmly under your belt, that's real power."

CLINT EASTWOOD

"Self-discipline is a form of freedom. Freedom from laziness and lethargy, freedom from the expectations and demands of others, freedom from weakness and fear—and doubt. Self-discipline allows a person to feel his individuality, his inner strength, his talent. He is master of, rather than a slave to, his thoughts and emotions."

H.A. DORFMAN

Thoughts/Actions:

319

"Everything we hear is an opinion, not a fact. Everything we see is a perspective, not the truth."

MARCUS AURELIUS

Don't take anything personal today. Do not let negative energy affect your day because everything we hear is an opinion, not a fact. Everything we see is a perspective, not the truth.

People's beliefs and opinions are formed on how they perceive their surroundings and by what they learn from others. Just because someone doesn't have the same beliefs as you doesn't mean one of you is wrong. It just means you've learned and perceived things differently.

For example, you have two babies born on the same day. One set of parents is told not to pick up their crying baby because they don't want to "spoil" their child. So they never pick up their baby when it cries in hopes of not spoiling it. The other set of parents is told to always pick up their baby when it cries and to nurture the baby as much as possible. These children will grow up perceiving the world completely different, and this is just the very beginning of their lives.

Thoughts/Actions:

320

"Every time you subtract negative from your life, you make room for more positive."

UNKNOWN

Thoughts/Actions:

321

"When you stop doing things for fun
you might as well be dead."

HEMINGWAY

Thoughts/Actions:

322

"If you can't see the bright side
of life, polish the dull side."

UNKNOWN

Thoughts/Actions:

323

Each morning, when you open your eyes, think
only three things: Thank you, Thank you, and
Thank you. Then, set out to make the best use of
the gift of this day that you can."

UNKNOWN

Being thankful increases your vibration. The
higher your vibration, the better you feel, and the
more good things you will effortlessly attract to

yourself. Be thankful for not only the "big" things in your life, but also for the simplest of joys.

Thoughts/Actions:

324

"Open your mouth only if what you are going to say is more beautiful than silence."

UNKNOWN

Thoughts/Actions:

325

"Do the best you can until you know better. Then when you know better, do better."

MAYA ANGELOU

The key is to do and be the best that you can...

Thoughts/Actions:

326

"You gotta look for the good in the bad, the happy in your sad, the gain in your pain, and what makes you grateful not hateful."

KAREN SALMANSOHN

Every moment is new. Be sure to make time for yourself/yoursoul today. Be deliberate in finding your joy. Be aware of and appreciative of all the little moments that bring you joy. For me, I've already had three joyful moments this morning. Seeing my children's beautiful faces, bird-watching (and listening), and a cup of delicious hot chocolate. Watch for, and appreciate the "little" moments that cause you to feel good.

And as you know, what you look for you get more of. So when you look for the good in the bad, the happy in your sad, the gain in your pain, and what makes you grateful not hateful, you will effortlessly attract more of the positive that you seek.

Have a beautiful, joyful, and grateful day.

Thoughts/Actions:

327

A philosophy professor asked his students just one question for their final exam.

The question was:
"How are you going to make me believe that this chair in front of you is invisible"?

It took all of the students hours to finish the exam with the exception of one lazy student who finished in 5 seconds. At the end of the day the test results were posted. The lazy student got the highest score. Know what his answer was?

"What chair?"

Lesson:
Do not make simple things complicated.

Thoughts/Actions:

328

"Depending on another person for your happiness is like using crutches in spite of having feet."

UNKNOWN

Thoughts/Actions:

329

"Live your life, and risk it all. Take some
chances, take the fall. Take your time,
no need to hurry. Have some fun, and
never worry. Live for the little things"

UNKNOWN

Thoughts/Actions:

330

"When you talk, you are only repeating
what you already know. But if you listen,
you may learn something new."

UNKNOWN

Thoughts/Actions:

331

"People inspire you, or they drain
you – pick them wisely."

HANS HANSEN

We get to choose, so choose wisely. And
remember the opposite is true as well. Be sure
you are inspiring others and not draining them.

Thoughts/Actions:

332

"People come into your life for a reason; the negative people usually are there to teach you what you don't want to become, treat you how you don't want to be treated, and to show you what you don't deserve. Embrace them, let them teach you, and then let them go."

ROXANNE HOFFNER

"Protect your spirit from contamination. Limit your time with negative people."

THEMA DAVIS

A powerful lesson. You can't know what you do want, until you experience what you don't want. Negative people are so draining. And it's not about blaming someone who is negative because most of the time negativity is a learned behavior. But it's in the learning, and in the letting go that allows for true inner peace and happiness. Here's to appreciating the lessons learned, for they've taught us what we don't want, and valuing ourselves enough to put an end to it once we realize it. Limit the time you spend with people who drain you in any way, or free yourself completely if possible. Ahhhhhh

Thoughts/Actions:

333

"Teaching a child not to step on
a caterpillar is as valuable to the
child as it is to the caterpillar."

UNKNOWN

"Show each person the courtesy to let them choose their way of life and their beliefs, then respect it, provided they do no harm to others, be it mankind, the animals or our Mother Earth."

E.C. MONTANA

Thoughts/Actions:

334

An anthropologist proposed a game to children of an African tribe. He put a basket full of fruit under a tree and he told children that the first one to reach the fruit would win them all. When he told them to run, they all took each other's hands and ran together, then they sat down together to enjoy the fruit. When asked why they ran like that, as one of them could have taken all the fruit for oneself, they said, "UBUNTU, how can one of us be happy if all the others are sad?" Ubuntu is a philosophy of African tribes that can be summed up as "I am because we are."

UNKNOWN

Thoughts/Actions:

335

"The most important trip you may take
in life is meeting people half way."

HENRY BOYLE

Thoughts/Actions:

336

"At the end of the day, the only questions I
will ask myself are... Did I love enough? Did
I laugh enough? Did I make a difference?"

KATRINA MAYER

Thoughts/Actions:

337

"Never blame anyone in your Life. Good people
give you Happiness. Bad people give you
Experience. Worst people give you a Lesson. And
Best people give you memories."

UNKNOWN

Be thankful for all you've crossed paths with.

Thoughts/Actions:

338

Today I am excited about everything!

"You have to be excited by a stone on the sidewalk or, like a child, the flight of a bird."

GABRIEL OROZCO

"Great is the man who has not lost his childlike heart."

MENCIUS

"You can be childlike without being childish. A child always wants to have fun. Ask yourself, Am I having fun?"

CHRISTOPHER MELONI

Thoughts/Actions:

339

"The amazing thing about life is that you choose what you allow into it, you choose how things affect you, you choose how you react. Happiness is a choice. Make it."

UNKNOWN

Thoughts/Actions:

340

KARMA

When people insult you, don't take offense, don't take it personally, but do listen to their words. They are telling you how they see the world, and they are telling you the exact negative qualities that they possess. "The Law of Mirrors" states that one can only see what's in them, regardless if it is what is actually present in reality or not. Release the need to defend or try to explain to them that you're not being whatever ~ nasty ~ insult ~ they've ~ thrown ~ at ~ you, but evaluate instead all of these insults, and realize that this is who they are. Then, decide if a person with those qualities is one who you'd like in your life or not.

DOE ZANTAMATA

When people insult you, lie to you, or disrespect you, don't take offense because it's about them not you. It's who they are, not who you are.

Thoughts/Actions:

341

"One of the hardest things in this world is to admit you are wrong. And nothing is more helpful in resolving a situation than its frank admission."

BENJAMIN DISRAELI

"When I look back on my life I can see the pain I've endured, the mistakes I've made and the hard times I've suffered. When I look in the mirror I see how strong I've become, the lessons I've learned and I'm proud of who I am."

DAVESWORDSOFWISDOM.COM

Thoughts/Actions:

342

"It turns out that the voice in our head is not a very good guide to life, and yet we tend to accept what it says and do what is suggests. This voice, in fact, is the cause of human suffering."

GINA LAKE

The good thing is we get to choose what the voice in our head is saying. With practice you can only tell yourself positive, loving thoughts in which everyone, including yourself will benefit.

And have fun with this! Because thinking good thoughts feel good!

Thoughts/Actions:

343

"You should sit in meditation for twenty minutes every day–unless you're too busy; then you should sit for an hour."

OLD ZEN ADAGE

Meditation doesn't have to be hard and it isn't. It's easy, inexpensive, and can be done anywhere. It can be as simple as going for a walk, being "in the flow" by doing something you love, repeating a word or phrase, focusing on your breath, putting on headphones and listening to an online guided meditation, etc. Whatever works for YOU, just as long as you quiet your mind for a few minutes a day. There is a ton of information available on meditation and the benefits are huge. Here's to inner peace, connecting with our inner-selves, and reducing stress. Here's a list with a few benefits.

Thoughts/Actions:

344

"I am coming to feel that the people of ill will have used time much more effectively than the people of good will. We will have to repent in this generation not merely for the vitriolic words and actions of the bad people but for the appalling silence of the good people."

MARTIN LUTHER KING JR.

Thoughts/Actions:

345

The World is Awakening

Can you feel it? They say there are only two emotions. Love and Fear. All other emotions, with which we are all so familiar, are nothing more than subcategories of these two. We were born as loving beings, and fear is something we've learned. Let's shake off the years and years of polluted programming that has made us feel separate from one another, that has taught us to create enemies instead of teaching us how to unite. Happiness is a choice, peace of mind is a choice, and Love is a choice. The world is awakening. Networking sites are full of examples and expressions of Love. ♥ There are so many family photos full of love; sons, daughters, moms, dads, nieces, nephews, aunts, uncles, grandchildren, grandparents, and great grandparents too. There are so many sincere and caring posts from not only friends but from strangers too, there are so many heartfelt birthday wishes, positive quotes, and photos capturing some of nature's great beauty. The list goes on and on. The world is awakening.

Thoughts/Actions:

346

How to Live a Blessed Life by
ANNA PEREIRA

Think happy thoughts.
Be thankful.
Wish others well
YES even your enemies.
Ignore what disrupts your Joy.
Focus on the positives
Every situation has one.
Pray.
Manifest your desires by whole heartedly believing in them and you.
Give love freely.

Thoughts/Actions:

347

"Don't criticize what you don't understand, son. You never walked in that man's shoes."

ELVIS PRESLEY

I love this quote. (And Elvis too!) I think learning how to end critical and judgmental thoughts leads to freedom. There is also a 100% chance that if you were to walk in someone else's shoes from day one, that you would make the same choices they have. So how can we ever fairly judge someone? We don't know how others were raised. We don't know if they were spoiled, neglected, abused, etc. We don't know what they've been taught, or what they haven't been taught. We don't know what they've experienced or how those experiences have shaped & molded them. We don't know how outside influences have affected them or how they have internally processed all of them. The list goes on and on. There is so much we don't know. We need to trust that everyone is learning and growing at their own pace and that it is all in perfect time.

Just because we can't understand why or how a person does what they do, doesn't give us the right to judge or criticize them. There is so much I don't understand about people and the reasons why they do the things they do. I just don't get it and I could drive myself crazy trying to figure it out. Heck, there are many things that I have done, and choices I have made that even I don't understand. There are times when I look back and wonder, what was I thinking?! Hence the saying "Hindsight is 20/20". I just have to trust that I am learning and growing, and that it's all part of the process.

Don't drive yourself crazy because you can't understand why someone else does what they do. It has nothing to do with you. You are never going to understand if you haven't walked in their shoes, which you haven't, so live and let live without having an opinion about it. Focus on yourself. Focus on growing and bettering YOU while trusting and enjoying the ride.

Thoughts/Actions:

348

"I hope your dreams stay big and
your worries stay small."
RASCAL FLATTS–MY WISH

Remember to relax, breathe, and let go...

Thoughts/Actions:

349

Every Day, Every Step, Every Breath, Every Choice, Every Walk, Every Bite, Every Climb, Every Moment, Every Opportunity, Every Comment, Every Life, Every Friend, Every Action, Every Kiss, Every Living being, Every Encounter, Every Hug, Every Second, Every Deed, Every Smile, Every Thought, Every Feeling , Every Hour, Every Dream, Every Rep , Every Day, Every Person MATTERS!

UNKNOWN

Make the most of everything, be deliberate with everything, and be aware of everything, because everything matters.

Thoughts/Actions:

350

"Reflect upon your blessings, of which every man has plenty, not on your past misfortunes, of which all men have some. "

CHARLES DICKENS

"Little minds are tamed and subdued by misfortune; but great minds rise above them."

WASHINGTON IRVING

You can't rise above your past misfortunes, if you keep talking about them. Appreciate "misfortunes" for what they've taught you and let them go... once and for all. Move forward towards something better.

Thoughts/Actions:

351

"To live happily ever AFTER
is to delay HAPPINESS.
Why not live happily forever NOW?"

DAVID CUSCHIERI

Have a happily ever after day
NOW... today and every day.

Thoughts/Actions:

352

Mathematics of Life

Life

+ Laughter

x Love

– Hate
_____

= Happiness

A simple math equation for you today. Have a happy day!

Thoughts/Actions:

353

To Each His Own
We Live & Learn
Trust and have faith in this, and
trust it for others as well.

"At the end of the game, pawns and
kings go back into the same box."

ITALIAN PROVERB

Thoughts/Actions:

354

What do you see?

*Big Mud Puddles and Sunny
Yellow Dandelions*

AUTHOR UNKNOWN

When I look at a patch of dandelions, I see a bunch of weeds that are going to take over my yard. My kids see flowers for Mom and blowing white fluff you can wish on.

When I look at an old drunk and he smiles at me, I see a smelly, dirty person who probably wants money and I look away. My kids see someone smiling at them and they smile back.

When I hear music I love, I know I can't carry a tune and don't have much rhythm so I sit self-consciously and listen. My kids feel the beat and move to it. They sing out the words. If they don't know them, they make up their own.

When I feel wind on my face, I brace myself against it. I feel it messing up my hair and pulling me back when I walk.

My kids close their eyes, spread their arms and fly with it, until they fall to the ground laughing.

When I pray, I say thee and thou and grant me this, give me that. My kids say, "Hi God! Thanks for my toys and my friends. Please keep the bad dreams away tonight. Sorry, I don't want to go to Heaven yet. I would miss my Mommy and Daddy."

When I see a mud puddle I step around it. I see muddy shoes and dirty carpets. My kids splash, dance, and sit in it. They see dams to build, rivers to cross, and worms to play with.

I wonder if we are given kids to teach or to learn from? No wonder God loves the little children! Enjoy the little things in life, for one day you may look back and realize they were the big things.

I wish you Big Mud Puddles and
Sunny Yellow Dandelions!!!

Thoughts/Actions:

355

"Let no man pull you so low as to hate him."
MARTIN LUTHER KING JR.

"I will permit no man to narrow and degrade my soul by making me hate him."
BOOKER T .WASHINGTON

Thoughts/Actions:

356

"Surrender to what is. Let go of what
was. Have faith in what will be."

SONIA RICOTTI

Thoughts/Actions:

357

"You can't make positive discoveries that make
your life better if you never try anything new."

JOSH KAUFMAN

Thoughts/Actions:

358

"A fool searches for the perfect life,
while a wise man makes the life he
has perfect." Jennifer Gayle

Thoughts/Actions:

359

"A great attitude becomes a great day which becomes a great month which becomes a great year which becomes a great LIFE."

MANDY HALE

Thoughts/Actions:

360

"Any intelligent fool can make things bigger, more complex, and more violent. It takes a touch a genius–and a lot of courage–to move in the opposite direction."

ALBERT EINSTEIN

Thoughts/Actions:

361

"Gratitude is absolutely the way to bring more into your life."

UNKNOWN

Gratitude for what you already have is the KEY to happiness and to bringing more good into your life. Has life got you down? Are you having a hard time being thankful for what you have? Why don't you:

- Take a cold shower every day for a week. At the end of the week, I bet you will be extremely thankful for warm water.

- Sleep on the floor or the ground for a week with no blankets. At the end of the week, I bet you will be extremely thankful for a soft bed to rest on and the comfort you get from a single blanket.

- Get two eye patches or a blindfold and cover your eyes for a week, or how about for one day? I bet after just 24 hours you will be thankful that you can see not only where you are going, but the beauty all around you.

- Put earplugs in and earmuffs on for an entire day. Usually hearing even the faintest sounds are taken for granted.

- Handcuff or tie your hands behind your back for a week, or just for one weekend. I bet you will be extremely thankful for your incredible hands when the weekend is over. (Heck, start out by wearing mittens, don't forget to have gratitude for your amazing fingers.)

These are just a few things that popped into my head, but the list goes on and on. Don't forget to be thankful for your food, clothing, and shelter;

lights, transportation, nature and especially for your loved ones.

To do any of the above would be challenging and you'd probably want to rip the blindfold off or untie your hands within the first five minutes, but it would remind you to be thankful for some of the basic things in life that we so often take for granted.

A lot of things in life can distract us from gratitude; the media, debt, disappointments, comparing ourselves to others and what others are doing, and constantly living a busy life without taking regular breaks to just be. Remember Theodore Roosevelt said "Comparison is the thief of joy."

Don't let life get you down! Be mindful of your thoughts. Be thankful! Come from gratitude and you will automatically attract more good things into your life because like attracts like. And it's unlimited! The more grateful you are, the more great things will come to you. It's like magic, but really it's just one of the laws of the Universe.

Have a grateful day!

Thoughts/Actions:

362

"A meaningful life is not being rich, being popular, being highly educated, or being perfect... It is about being real, being humble, being strong, and being able to share ourselves and touch the lives of others... It is only then that we could have a full, happy and contented life."

MAR RAZALAN

Thoughts/Actions:

363

"I am not bound to win, but I am bound to be true. I am not bound to succeed, but I am bound to live by the light that I have. I must stand with anybody that stands right, and stand with him while he is right, and part with him when he goes wrong."

ABRAHAM LINCOLN

Thoughts/Actions:

364

"Not to spoil the ending for you, but
everything is going to be OK!"

UNKNOWN

Have peace in knowing this. And
allow yourself to trust it.

Thoughts/Actions:

365

Our life is a book. "We will open the book. Its
pages are blank. We are going to put words on
them ourselves. The book is called Opportunity
and its first chapter is New Year's Day."

EDITH LOVEJOY PIERCE

Afterword

"You must unlearn what you have been programmed to believe since birth. That software no longer serves you if you want to live in a world where all things are possible."
JACQUELINE E. PURCELL

The intention of this book is to keep things simple and to provoke thought and action; to empower you on your journey and to remind you of your strength. When you make it a habit to incorporate positive changes into your life, one day at a time, you will reap many benefits. Live in the present, and appreciate each day while moving forward towards your dreams and goals... one baby step at a time. We are meant to love, have fun, and dream big!

Other titles by Find Your Way Publishing:
- Always Within; Grieving the Loss of Your Infant
- Guaranteed Success for Kindergarten; 50 Easy Things You Can Do Today!
- Guaranteed Success for Grade School; 50 Easy Things You Can Do Today!
- The Secret Combination to Middle School; Real Advice from Real Kids, Ideas for Success, and Much More!
- Prank and Pray You Get Away! - Over 60 Fun Jokes to Play on Your Sibling
- I Love You 1000 Times plus Infinity
- I Miss You 1000 Times plus Infinity
- I'm Sorry 1000 Times plus Infinity
- I Love You 1000 Times plus Infinity - Pocket Edition
- I Miss You 1000 Times plus Infinity - Pocket Edition
- I'm Sorry 1000 Times plus Infinity - Pocket Edition
- Congratulations 1000 Times plus Infinity - Pocket Edition

About
Melissa Eshleman

Melissa lives in Maine with her husband, Ed. After the death of their infant son, Lucas, their lives changed dramatically. Lucas died in their arms on May 20, 2001, and during his last hours he showed his love in amazing ways. Within a year Melissa quit her full-time job as an Office Manager for a global corporation, to be a stay-at-home mom to their children. The decision was a frightening one and required a life-style change for their entire family, but in Melissa's heart it was a decision that did not require logical thinking. On paper they didn't know how they were going to survive financially without the additional income. They not only became aware of their spending, but they also became aware of a precious thing called "time".

Melissa found comfort and support through an on-line infant-loss group. For the first year after Lucas' death, she read other people's stories and found that she wasn't alone in her grief. As time passed she found that she was helping others with her words and realized that she was healing through the process. It was then that Melissa realized she wanted to publish books to help others, not only with their grief but also by partnering with others to help people grow in all areas of their lives.

Other titles by Melissa:
Always Within; Grieving the Loss of Your Infant

Disclaimer

The purpose of this book is for entertainment purposes only. The author and Find Your Way Publishing, Inc. shall have neither liability nor responsibility to any person or entity with respect to any loss or damage caused, or alleged to have been caused, directly or indirectly, by the information contained in this book. If you do not wish to be bound by the above, you may return this book along with a copy of the receipt to the publisher for a full refund.

Index

A Quote a Day to Find Your Way

Quotes & Thoughts to Inspire You on Your Journey

Quick Order Form

Fax orders:
207-514-0438.
Please send this form with your order.

Telephone orders:
207-514-0575

Internet orders:
www.findyourwaypublishing.com

Postal orders:
Find Your Way Publishing, Inc.
PO Box 667
Norway, ME 04268
USA

Please include:
    Name of book:
    Quantity:
    Your Name:
    Address:
    City:
    State:
    Zip:
    Telephone:
    Email address: